***POWERFUL** Partnerships*®

POWERFUL *Partnerships*

The Power to Transform Any Relationship Into a Great One!

by Dr. Jim Goldstein

Powerful Partnerships®
The Power to Transform Any Relationship into a Great One

DR. JIM GOLDSTEIN

©2010 by DR. JIM GOLDSTEIN
All Rights Reserved. Printed in the United States

No part of this book may be reproduced, stored in or introduced into a retrieval system, or transmitted, in any form or by any means – electronic, mechanical, photocopying, recording or otherwise – without the prior written permission of the copyright owner.

ISBN: 1453712542 and EAN-13 is 9781453712542

Credits

Cover and Book design by Sandra Larson
www.SLDWEB.com

DEDICATION

This book is dedicated to my wife, Lauren, the love of my life and my greatest source of inspiration. It is also dedicated to my children, Thea and Todd, who taught me what it means to be powerful.

POWERFUL *Partnerships*®
www.drjimgoldstein.com/site/free-bonus

ACKNOWLEDGMENTS

I want to acknowledge and thank the many friends and colleagues who made this book possible. First, I want to thank my wife, Lauren, for her patience with me as I experimented with different ways of expressing myself and for her partnership and support over the past 28 years. Everything I recommend to couples was first tested on her. Because of her, I know these things work. I also want to thank my brother, Marty Goldstein, for challenging some of my assumptions and helping me to gain clarity about what is essential for a successful relationship. Throughout my life, I have been blessed to have the support and inspiration of my sister, Nancy Ross and her husband, Alan. My children, Thea and Todd, gave me the greatest gift at an early age by demonstrating how quickly and easily they could resolve their differences even before they had a sophisticated grasp of language. I credit them for my creation of the Four-Channel Clearing™.

I also want to thank Brad Blanton for teaching me the value of expressing both resentments and appreciations in the formation and healing of intimate relationships. He taught me to pay attention to the sensations in my body and to express my feelings, no matter how uncomfortable, rather than act them out. I also want to thank Lethia Owens for helping me to establish my personal brand and for encouraging me to finish this project and get it out to the world.

Many people had a hand in editing this manuscript. I especially want to thank Marita O'Connell, Sarah Jackson, Sallie Boyles, Becky Weiss, Ruth Handelsman, Duane Sylvia and Steve Dorfman for their valuable input.

I greatly appreciate Sandra Larson for taking the edited manuscript and, through her creative design and sensible layout, turning it into what I hope is an easy to read and valuable book.

Finally, I want to acknowledge my parents, Gene and Roslyn Goldstein for modeling a loving relationship and giving me a blueprint for a happy marriage.

Contents

DEDICATION . . . . *v*

ACKNOWLEDGMENTS . . . . *vii*

INTRODUCTION 13

CHAPTER 1
Basic Premises of the Powerful Partnerships Program. 18

CHAPTER 2
Power, Force, and Structure. 28

CHAPTER 3
Love Never Requires Sacrifice. 60

CHAPTER 4
How To Determine What Is True. 75

CHAPTER 5
Intimacy and Boundaries. 92

CHAPTER 6
Modeling Children's Behavior. 97

CHAPTER 7
Why Punishment Doesn't Work in Relationships 106

CHAPTER 8

Context versus Content *112*

CHAPTER 9

Four Channels of Truth. *116*

CHAPTER 10

Setting the Stage for The Four-Channel Clearing *148*

CHAPTER 11

The Four-Channel Clearing In Action *152*

CHAPTER 12

What to Do and What to Say
When You Realize You Are Upset. *164*

CHAPTER 13

Regenerating and Recreating Love. *174*

CHAPTER 14

Staying Connected *178*

CHAPTER 15

The Courage to Feel *182*

CHAPTER 16

Why We Want What We Want *199*

CHAPTER 17

The Limits of Powerful Partnerships. *204*

POWERFUL *Partnerships*®
www.drjimgoldstein.com/site/free-bonus

CHAPTER 18

Achieving Mastery in Your Relationships
Through Powerful Partnerships *211*

CHAPTER 19

Powerful Partnerships Beyond
the Committed Relationship *220*

CHAPTER 20

Putting It All Together *223*

GLOSSARY *229*

ABOUT THE AUTHOR *237*

INTRODUCTION

Across from me sit two people, married, no longer feeling close to each other. Why they're still together, aside from their commitment to their children, they don't know. They say that sex is okay when it happens, but it doesn't happen often.

"Helen", I ask, "What could Richard do to make you feel loved?"

"He could bring me flowers when it's not Mother's Day or some holiday."

"Did you know she would like that, Richard?" I ask.

"Yes, I know she loves roses."

"Do you ever do that, just bring her roses for no special reason?"

"No"

"Do you love Helen?"

"Yes, I do."

"If you know she loves roses, why don't you ever bring her any?"

"I don't know."

When Richard says, "I don't know," he really means it. People often don't know where the love went or why it diminished over time. Without any intervention, this relationship probably won't get better over time; it will deteriorate. By the time a couple reaches this stage, they feel a sense of resignation and are more likely to settle for those fleeting remembrances of the intimacy that once bound them together.

Consider, if you will, another example. Have you ever observed an elderly couple walking hand in hand, shoulders touching, heads inclined towards one another? Instead of age spots and sagging skin, he sees the rosy-cheeked beauty he first met; she sees the strapping young man who swept her off her feet. Their love is ageless. Time, in fact, has made it more profound and even sweeter.

How did they create such an intimate, lasting love affair? What makes love stay rather than fade over time?

After studying couples in and out of my private practice for over 20 years, and also going through the ups and downs of my own 28-year marriage, I discovered something that profoundly impacted my understanding of relationships. I now know exactly what erodes the good feelings we used to have and what restores the love that was once there. More importantly, I know what to do and what not to do to transform any relationship into a great one.

Consequently, I developed the *Powerful Partnerships®* program so that you may gain the understanding and the tools to achieve the kind of relationship you've always wanted.

My program focuses on two main areas:

1) a way of being with your partner, and

2) a special kind of communication that, over time, gives you the freedom to express and enjoy the love you used to feel when you and your partner were first dating.

Couples who have given up on feeling passion again can turn their relationships around to a degree that is nothing short of remarkable. In fact, here's what you can expect if you practice the principles of *Powerful Partnerships®*:

1. Without necessarily understanding why, you'll find yourself pleasing your partner again simply because you want to.

2. You'll feel acknowledged, appreciated and valued for the things you do.

3. When you feel upset, you'll be able to know exactly what is bothering you, and then express

your feelings in ways that heal you without arousing defensiveness, resistance or argument in your partner.

4. You'll learn how to clean up any old hurts that are still unresolved without requiring your partner to admit anything, apologize or promise to be different.

5. If you get stuck in an uncomfortable place with your partner, you'll know exactly what to say to get back on the same team quickly. Over time, you'll find that you become stuck less often, and when those situations arise, they don't last as long as they used to.

6. You'll develop the power to get what you want without having to resort to manipulation, guilt, anger, or any type of force. Love will become the only legitimate motivator in your relationship.

7. As a result of practicing *Powerful Partnerships*®, you will swear that your partner's physical appearance has improved. Whether or not this is empirically true, your beloved will become more physically attractive to you, even if you can't explain why. Love does that.

All the tools to create the relationship you've always wanted are here for you in this book. They don't offer an instant cure or a quick fix. However, as soon as you practice these skills, your relationship will begin to move in a better direction and that will inspire you to keep at it.

Believe it or not, the love you once felt is still there, alive and well, waiting to be released!

Consistently, people who learn and practice *Powerful Partnerships*® say the program is unlike anything else they have tried. Therefore, I invite you to put aside any assumptions you may have regarding interpersonal communication or couples therapy. Simply be open to new perspectives on your partner, yourself and all your relationships. If you are willing to move forward in this way, you will be gratified by the changes you've been able to bring about in your life.

CHAPTER **1**

Basic Premises of the *Powerful Partnerships* Program

What you will learn from this chapter:

How to transform even the most difficult relationships through self-expression

We are about to delve into some underlying presuppositions about the way human beings relate to each other, and how they can achieve happiness.

1. Nothing external to you (including your spouse, partner, parents, siblings, coworkers, or situation) has to change for you to feel happy and fulfilled.

2. Self-expression changes the way you feel, releasing you from the expectation that things have to be different for you to be happy.

3. Self-expression is powerful; the most powerful way to express yourself is to tell the truth.

4. People in relationships generally want to please each other.

5. Love is the only legitimate motivator in a relationship.

Some of the premises might seem hard for you to believe. Even if you question the validity, consider each one. By keeping an open mind, you are likely to gain insights that present a clearer understanding of others and yourself.

Nothing external to you—not your spouse, partner, parents, siblings, coworkers, or situation—has to change for you to feel happy and fulfilled.

How fantastic would it be if everyone around you suddenly started behaving exactly the way you wanted? While you might daydream about how much more pleasurable such a life might be, you will soon understand that these things don't have to happen for you to feel happy and satisfied. In fact, nothing external to you—not your spouse, partner, parents, siblings, coworkers, or situation—has to change for you to feel happy and fulfilled.

Basic Premises of the Powerful Partnerships Program

It's quite natural to complain about people or conditions external to you, convincing yourself that you are absolutely stuck if those external elements don't change. However, having that frame of mind places you at the self-inflicted mercy of things beyond your control. *Powerful Partnerships®* shows you how to transform your experience whether anyone or anything around you changes. In effect, you will learn to act rather than being reactive to external forces.

Self-expression changes the way you feel, releasing you from the expectation that things have to be different for you to be happy.

Why is it important to express yourself? Self-expression changes the way you feel and releases you from the expectation that things have to be different for you to be happy. Self-expression, in fact, gives you the power to heal all wounds. As you express yourself truthfully, the wounds you've collected lose their emotional charge and a natural healing process takes place. By changing yourself you will further enable those around you to change naturally.

Think about a time when you talked honestly about something that bothered you. After you got it off your chest, do you recall feeling less troubled? *Powerful Partnerships®* unlocks that sense of peace and power. Self-expression transforms your experience.

You might wonder about the wisdom of being totally honest. Can't honesty be hurtful? Absolutely! To go into a person's house and exclaim, "What a dump!" might be honest. It can easily be perceived as hurtful, too. It's often not what you say, but how you say it that feels hurtful. *Powerful Partnerships®* will empower you to tell the truth in ways that are healing.

For years, my wife used to criticize the informal clothing I wore when I met clients. "Wearing Birkenstock sandals makes you look like Fred Flintstone!" she complained at one point. In response, I argued that I didn't need to be a fashion plate. "People who come to me are interested in what I have to say, not in my shoes," I retorted.

In honestly expressing her opinion, my wife did not motivate me to wear more businesslike attire. Instead, she provoked defensiveness and stubbornness in me. In fact, I was more determined than ever to dress as I pleased. However, after learning about *Powerful Partnerships®*, she altered her approach.

"I think that you are a wise man, and many people benefit from hearing what you have to say," she began. "It could be that your tee shirts and jeans don't matter to younger clients, but it would be a waste if the older ones, perhaps a young client's parents, were not able to take in what you were saying just because they couldn't get past the ripped knees of your pants. It's your practice and you can do what you want, but I would like for you to dress like a professional so that you reach everyone."

That time her words touched me. My wife conveyed that she respected my professional capabilities, and, therefore, wanted me to consider how important it was for my clients to perceive my value. Presented in that manner, the truth in her message came across as a helpful suggestion, not as an attack. I soon started wearing dress slacks and a button-down shirt for all of my client meetings.

Self-expression is powerful.
The most powerful way to express
yourself is to tell the truth.

When children are upset, they need to express themselves before they can feel better. As a rule, they don't keep much inside. When distressed, they typically speak and react quickly and genuinely without holding back. While what they say and do might seem inappropriate at times, getting it all out enables children to return to their formerly happy state. Their ability to recover their natural state of happiness through self-expression is part of what makes them so powerful. From young children I have learned that self-expression is powerful, and that the most powerful way to express yourself is to tell the truth.

Over time, we as adults lose the ability to be expressive. We don't know how to release our emotions in order to heal from the situations that upset us. Why? Some of us were shamed or punished for speaking too openly or at inappropriate times, so we learned to keep our feelings inside. Even if we were never admonished for communicating our emotions, we might have found that our attempts to be honest sometimes backfired and made conditions worse. In either case, if we decide that it's not safe to be open, we diminish our capacity to heal. With that attitude, we tend to harbor resentments and hurts. Ultimately, without honest self-expression, we hinder self-love and the expressions of love and forgiveness from thriving in our relationships.

If two people stop wanting to please one another, most likely, someone, somewhere did not communicate something truthfully. Even after you have reached this juncture, telling the truth can restore the original warmth you shared and your desire to please.

People in relationships generally want to please each other.

Imagine that you have invited new friends to your home as guests. Following convention, you might ask if they'd like some coffee. If they accept, you would predictably ask if anyone likes sugar or cream. If someone indicates a liking for three spoonfuls of sugar and a dash of cream, you are probably going to prepare the cup in that manner. Why? Clearly, you would want to please your new friends!

The desire to please is a natural tendency in all relationships. If possible, then, you want to make the other person in your relationship happy. Interestingly, however, that inclination changes after an extended commitment or marriage.

Burt, for instance, has a belly. Even though his wife, Sue, knows he'd like three sugars in his coffee she says to herself, "He doesn't need all that sugar" and only puts in one cube!

Instead of intervening in a controlling manner, *Powerful Partnerships®* provides a way to replace the penchant to manipulate your partner with your innate desire to please. The process begins by learning how to tell your partner the truth. When you gain the freedom to release your resentments, your natural desire to please will return. How?

You will regain access to the kindness and thoughtfulness inside—even if those elements have been hidden for years. You will find that you want to please your partner much the way you did when you first met.

That example presents a question that people frequently ask me: *Don't you think we please people because we want them to like us?*

The answer, I believe, is that as we get older, our motivations shift from wanting to please to wanting to be liked and to look good in other people's eyes.

Consider, for instance, how you feel and act around babies. Babies elicit a willingness to please that is not based on trying to look good in the baby's eyes or wanting the baby's approval. When you connect with such a pure little being, your instinct is to support and nurture him or her out of love, with little regard to what you might get in return. It is in the giving that you receive gratification.

In regards to the same question about motivation, I also believe that most new relationships begin with you having hope that the other person is good and that you can build a connection that is not based solely on what you can get out of it or what he or she can do for you. And, of course, it does feel good to please another, especially if the person shows appreciation.

Remember the wife who wanted flowers from her husband? Imagine how the relationship might benefit if she received a big bouquet for "no reason," and responded by giving him a hug and expressing words of gratitude. "Thank you for the flowers. They are beautiful! What a special way to surprise me!"

Love is the only legitimate motivator in a relationship.

In the early stage of a relationship, we do what we do out of love. We love to be with our partner, we love to do things with him or her, and we love being able to please the other when we can. Even if we are doing something that isn't what we'd choose to do if we were alone, we are happy to do it if we are feeling love. This is the foundation for our relationship and it is still the best reason for doing what we do vis-à-vis our partner.

As conditions progress (or regress) in a relationship, our motivation often changes. We may act out of obligation or guilt. We may act because we feel we should or we have to. We may act in ways to prove something to our partner, to be right, or for spite.

For the most part, these motivations will not lead to a good outcome with regard to how we feel about our partner. Even if we do the right things (something kind or considerate) for the wrong reasons (because we feel forced), we ultimately won't be fulfilled in our relationship.

Powerful Partnerships® is about getting us back in touch with the love that first motivated us. It is about establishing love as the only legitimate motivator of our behavior toward our partner. This often requires us to examine our own lives and find where the love and joy is inside us. The happier we are, the easier it is to be loving and kind and to feel love and compassion for our partner. It's less a matter of finding happiness than removing the blockages to our innate joy so that our natural love (that we had as a child) is able to come forth and be felt. *Powerful Partnerships*® will show you how to remove those impediments to happiness.

CHAPTER **2**

Power, Force, and Structure

What you will learn from this chapter:

How to enhance relationships by identifying force and replacing it with power

Love Never Dies

One of the premises of *Powerful Partnerships*® is that the love you once felt for your partner is alive and well and waiting to be experienced again. It may be suppressed and hidden but it is not dead. The original feelings you had should not be dismissed as romantic infatuation. The love you felt then was real and can be recreated under the right circumstances. A major part of *Powerful Partnerships*® is about increasing the access you have to the love inside yourself and allowing that love to color how you feel about your relationship.

Falling in love and having your heart broken

When you first meet someone and that attraction is there, what is really happening is that you are giving yourself permission to access the love inside yourself. It may look like the other person is making you feel this way and having this effect on you, but they aren't. What you are feeling is a connection to your Source or your inner being, an infinite supply of love, energy, joy and positive expectation and it feels fantastic. Love is a wonderful thing no matter what triggers it.

What follows after falling in love is pretty predictable. The more love and attraction you feel, the more open you become to this person. You feel happy a lot of the time. Again, what you are opening up to is the source of love inside you. You look forward to seeing them again, finding out more about them and having them get to know you. What could be better?

Then, when your defenses are down and your heart is open, this person invariably will violate your boundaries in some way, often without meaning to. Something they do or say, or neglect to do or say, won't meet your expectations and the first upset occurs. I call this, "the first glitch" and it is a very significant part of the life of a relationship. How you handle the first few glitches determines whether or not you even have a future with each other. If the glitches happen before you are in a committed relationship and aren't handled well, then they might mark the beginning of the end of the relationship. The eventual break-up can often be traced back to these early unresolved glitches.

If you get to the commitment stage of a relationship, there are even more expectations of your partner and more ways to be disappointed. Your ability to handle glitches, mistakes and missteps is even more crucial then because you have promised to stay with this person in front of witnesses. It won't be as easy to walk away the way you could if you were dating. This situation makes many people feel stuck when things begin to go badly. The heartbreak of the glitch is twofold; first, we no longer feel safe to be ourselves the way we did at first with this person and, second, we come to believe that we aren't going to be loved unconditionally the way we had hoped.

Adjusting to love's disappointments

Since you can't leave, you handle your anxiety, fears and disappointments in a number of ways. One is to lower your expectations about love. You may become more philosophical and reflective about those early emotions. Perhaps you can convince yourself that what you first felt was just infatuation. *Love of that intensity isn't supposed to last. I was being unrealistic. It's easy to feel that way when you have no history with a person, etc.*

Another way to handle the disappointment is to get busy - busy with life, busy with the kids, busy with school or work, busy with projects, busy with hobbies. By being too busy to talk, to appreciate each other or to be loving, we undermine our chances of intimacy even further.

Once things start to break down and love isn't our chief motivator, we resort to controlling behaviors to get what we want. Control can be exerted in many ways; money, sex, the silent treatment, getting sick, making *quid pro quo* deals *(I'll do this for you but you owe me that other thing next time).*

If we are still unable to get what we want, we often end up attacking our partner, showing them how wrong they are, talking about them to our friends, or generally bemoaning the inherent unfairness of our situation to whomever will listen.

Each way of interacting erodes the love and passion we once felt. Is it any wonder that people believe that true love doesn't last?

Powerful Partnerships® will help you to see where the blockages to love are. You are about to learn how interacting in a certain way opens up the flow of love and interacting in other ways tends to shut this flow off.

What Does It Mean to Have a Powerful Partnership?

It has been said that marriage is the ultimate psychotherapy. The covenant definitely offers an opportunity for psychological healing, emotional maturity and spiritual growth that you may not find elsewhere.

Most, especially those with good relationships, say that achieving a good marriage isn't easy—it takes work. That has been my experience as well. The work you do on your marriage, if done right, is rewarding and a long relationship where love is still strong is quite an accomplishment.

Why do you suppose achieving a happy, strong marriage is so hard?

Connection vs. Freedom

One reason might be that your committed relationship catches you in a bind. On one hand, you have an innate longing to connect with another person. Yet as much as you might want to be with someone, you may also want to feel free. No one wants to feel coerced or face limited choices. Meanwhile, a committed relationship requires that you not only be aware of what you want, but you must also consider your partner before making decisions that might affect him or her.

There's the rub. How can you be happy if you aren't free in a relationship to do whatever you wish?

The answer: *Powerful Partnerships*®. A powerful partnership gives you the intimate loving connection you want while safeguarding your freedom at the same time. It allows you the freedom to please your partner by doing what the other wishes because you *want to*—not because you *have to*. If what you desire conflicts with what your partner wants, rather than just complying or doing what you want regardless of the other's objections, a powerful partnership goes for a win-win solution. Above all, a powerful partnership sees love—not fear, guilt or manipulation—as the underlying foundation of the relationship. When you feel love, you are free to do what your partner wants you to do. Having that choice allows you to express your love willingly and cheerfully and brings you more intimacy. Additionally, the love that first existed in your relationship is likely hidden under much of what I call *force*.

How to Recognize Force

Let's define what force is in the context of a relationship. When you are on the receiving end of force, it doesn't feel good. Force makes you feel fearful, attacked, shamed, humiliated, embarrassed, manipulated, coerced, pressured, guilty, wrong, stupid, foolish, isolated, or defensive. If you find yourself thinking you *should, ought to, need to, have to,* or *must*, you are experiencing a kind of self-imposed force. Force also applies to feeling threatened. Clearly, if someone says or implies that you must do what he or she says *or else*, you'd likely experience the element of *force.*

Because force is subjective, intent is not the issue. Force is not determined by whether you *meant* to use it. The important question is: *Did the recipient feel it?* Maybe you didn't mean to force someone, but the individual felt forced from your tone of voice or use of words. Perception is the key. Why?

You and I filter what we hear based on our past experiences. Two people could hear the same thing from another person at the same time yet have completely opposite reactions to what was said. I might feel force and you might not feel it at all.

I once had a female client who tended to be highly distractible and forgetful. Her tendencies went well beyond her behavior in her marriage. After learning about the distinction, force, in her sessions with me, she told me that she felt force in her interactions at home with her husband. For instance, she recalled saying to him, "Honey, where did you want the boxes to go?" He replied, "I told you. They go in the bottom right drawer of the cabinet." Though his tone was

POWERFUL *Partnerships*®
www.drjimgoldstein.com/site/free-bonus

cheerful, his choice of words, which subtly suggested that she was in the wrong, made her feel diminished.

Another person in a similar situation might hear only the positive tone of voice. If her husband's phrasing didn't bother my client, then we wouldn't attempt to change anything. (Don't fix what isn't broken!) Since my client was upset, the couple's communication was worth examining. In the end, we realized that three words—*I told you*—were at the heart of the matter. His replies repeatedly began with *I told you*. In response, she felt as though she *should have* remembered this or *should not have* needed to ask that.

The fix was simple. Her husband simply needed to answer as though he had not told her before. *The boxes go in the bottom right drawer of the cabinet.* Hearing him respond in that way, she could put the boxes where they belonged without the residue of force.

Meanwhile, it turned out that her husband felt as though he was constantly repeating himself, so we determined how he could address his frustration: *I feel like I am often repeating myself with you. You don't have to do this, but I'd like for you to work on listening better if you can. I'll work on making sure you understood me the first time. Okay?*

Power, Force, and Structure

The distinction in phrasing might seem insignificant, but the choice of words can have a huge impact. In this situation, by removing the force from his sentences, the husband found that his wife was more willing to take on helpful tasks at home. If he had left *I told you* in his repertoire, she would have eventually lost her desire to please him. Additionally, she probably would have made a decision, perhaps subconsciously, to stop helping him.

Force Arises from Weakness—Not from Strength

By and large, we tend to use force when we feel powerless.

What would happen if you knew you could bring about the result you wanted through the power of effectively communicating? Why would you ever yell, threaten, pout, pitch a tantrum, withdraw love, use sarcasm, or employ overt violence or passive-aggressive behavior (force) to achieve results? Why would anyone manipulate another with shame, guilt, or logic if simply asking worked better?

It's sad, but the belief and suspicion that our needs are not going to be met often suppresses our innate desire to please. Consequently, instead of pleasing, we focus on how we might get others to do what we want through manipulation—a vote of no confidence in both our own worthiness and our partner's unconditional love for us.

Most young children, for example, love their grandparents unconditionally. You can easily imagine little ones running to greet Grandma and Grandpa with hugs and kisses. Over time, however, the dynamics often change. I've observed grandparents when they present special treats to their grandkids. Along with the gift came an expectation of some sort. Giving became a kind of barter. It's easy to imagine Grandma holding a gift behind her back while asking, "Where's my kiss? Where's my hug?" Does Grandma believe she won't get affection if she doesn't have something of value to trade? No matter what she feels, the child learns that love is a trade-off when it need not be. It didn't start out that way.

I've found an interesting paradox regarding power and force. Here it is: Force is actually weakness masquerading as strength. Conversely, power is strength often masquerading as weakness. One of the most powerful figures in American history was Abraham Lincoln. His power was often mistaken for weakness. He was routinely underestimated by his peers. His strength came through in his ability to forgive and be gentle with his detractors, his sense of humor, his focus on a vision he wanted to fulfill for America, his patience and determination in achieving his goals, and his ability to see more in a person than they were currently showing him. He almost single-handedly changed the entire country in four years. *That's powerful.*

Force is actually weakness often masquerading as strength

Force Begets Force

Using force in a relationship has consequences. Yes, you can make your partner comply with your wishes, but if you do that, over time, using force will have a corrosive effect on love, passion and spontaneity. Additionally, force does not go unanswered. Sooner or later force begets force, which begets more force. On and on, the spiral continues. Cut someone off in traffic and see what happens. Your aggressive move may evoke and an aggressive hand gesture in response followed by loud horn honking, dangerous tailgating or even road rage.

With couples, one person's mean-spirited criticism might be answered with aloofness (the big chill). Pushing the matter further, someone chooses to disappear for a while unannounced, so the other decides to sleep in a separate bedroom. The next morning, the person who usually makes lunches doesn't bother to fix a sandwich for his or her partner. During the day, there's no communication. Topping off the dissention, someone arrives home extremely late without explanation.

The presence of force can also hang in the air even if it plays out in a passive-aggressive manner. Let's say that a mom forces her daughter to practice the piano. As the girl progresses, demonstrating skill and talent, the mom may believe that her method produces terrific results.

It is possible to create a great pianist from this type of parenting. However, we've all encountered the person who took piano lessons for eight years during childhood but won't go near a piano because she has no love for playing as an adult. If she does sit down to play, it's always the same insipid tune. Such behavior is often a response to having been forced to practice as a child.

People who act this way rarely make an overt statement to the pushy parent: *I'll never touch the piano to get you back for all the time you made me practice. I hated those stupid lessons and I always felt forced to go. Now you can see that you wasted all your money on them since I won't touch the keyboard.* Instead, they show no interest in the instrument. Force begets force.

I was among the countless children who have been forced by their parents to take piano lessons. I had a strict teacher who shamed me weekly for my "atrocious scales." I hated practicing and never showed any particular talent. The entire experience was colored by force to the point that shame, resentment and resistance replaced my initial joy over making music. My parents allowed me to quit in fifth grade.

In the eighth grade, however, I had a chance to join a band. Without anyone forcing me, I began to pick out tunes on the piano by ear, and over time I became better and better at it. Soon I could play by ear any music I heard on the radio. I loved playing. I practiced for hours all through my college years, seeking pianos in empty practice rooms and learning more and more songs. I often was amazed at my own ability to stay with it as long as I did, but I recognized that my talent surfaced because I was doing what I wanted without pressure.

I worked with one couple with many issues of force in their relationship. The wife made her husband wrong for not making enough income. He was a gifted architect and builder but never seemed to turn a profit. She loved ballroom dancing and urged him to take lessons with her. During the lessons she was frustrated that he wasn't a good dancer and corrected him on the dance floor. Quite predictably, he made less and less money. He further resisted her invitations to go dancing. After they were divorced, however, he designed and renovated three historical buildings, which yielded an $800,000 profit. In addition, he took up swing dancing on his own and became an avid dancer. I'm not making this up!

Another example of force begetting force is a personal story. When I was younger, my brother and I were responsible for cutting the grass. We had an electric lawn mower with a thick cord that always got in the way. We didn't enjoy mowing with this heavy contraption, and constantly complained to my father about the cord. Nevertheless, my father refused to buy a gas mower. As I remember it, my brother, who especially hated this chore, managed to sever the cord with the lawn mower. I don't believe my brother or I consciously set out to cut the electrical cord, but we cut it repeatedly. In turn, my father was forced to repair it before the grass could be cut again. Force begets force.

Distinguishing Force from Structure

In a work setting, employers can insist that employees follow rules and procedures, and behave in a particular way. In fact, employees agree to abide by rules when they accept a job. No one can require them to remain employed there. Still, if workers must arrive at 8:30 or get fired, isn't that force?

My answer is, *No.* Such ground rules provide structure. The employer is saying, *You don't have to work here, but if you do, this is how we all play.*

Within the given structure, however, the application of power can radically transform the work experience for both the employee and the employer. Instead of bossing people around with a "because I said so" attitude (force), an employer can express his vision for the company and get people excited about fulfilling that vision. Instead of collecting evidence of repeated employee mistakes, an employer can focus on what people are doing right and acknowledge and appreciate them not just for what they are doing but for the ideas and critical thinking skills they have developed. Performance and productivity improves when people feel appreciated even within the non-negotiable structure of the workplace.

Structure also applies to an intimate relationship. Consider the following conversation that might take place before committing to marriage.

> Woman: *If we get married, my deal is this— you can't have sex with anyone else, and you can't hit me, no matter what.*
>
> Man: (thinking about the power-force distinction) *Hey! Aren't you **forcing** me to be*

> monogamous and exercise restraint no matter how nasty or annoying you get?

The answer is, *No*. She is not exerting force, but establishing structure by stating the conditions under which she is willing to get married. If he doesn't like the conditions, he can either negotiate something different or opt out. Moreover, coexisting within the agreed upon framework will yield power to both. The limitations that they have agreed to abide by will require more creativity, self-expression, and collaboration to arrive at a win-win solution. Engaging in these kinds of conversations and resolving the conflict will increase intimacy, trust, understanding, teamwork, appreciation and love.

Changing the Dance

As we said previously, *Powerful Partnerships*® is based partly on the premise that people in relationships—especially new ones—want to please each other. If that element is missing, most likely, at least one party is feeling force. You might have heard the interaction of a couple described as a *dance*. In a dance, a move by one partner leads to a corresponding move by the other. Over time, you can unwittingly dance with your partner in ways that conceal or suppress the previously generous, giving, attentive, or humorous side of him or her.

While working with one couple, I listened to the wife say how unromantic the husband was. In a somewhat resigned, wistful tone of voice she said, "I just have to accept the fact that John is not the romantic type. It's no big deal, really. He has so many other fine qualities that I should be grateful for." Later, when I met with John, he said, "I can't believe that she thinks I'm not romantic. I've always thought of myself as hopelessly romantic. I used to write handwritten cards to my girlfriends with poetry inside and take hours drawing artwork on the front." In the dance with his wife, however, that romantic side hadn't manifested itself for a long time. John was not "just that way," as his wife concluded; instead, the dance they had adopted precluded his romantic side from ever surfacing.

You may conclude, as the wife did above, that your partner isn't giving, doesn't love you, has not listened to you, or doesn't care about you anymore. If you are willing, however, to change the steps in the dance you do with your partner, you may see him or her from an entirely new perspective. Your partner might show you something you never thought he or she was capable of.

A Few New Steps

You might be concerned about how you might "sell" this program to your partner. *Do both of us have to agree to change for this to work?* Happily, the answer is *No.* Changing your relationship does not require your partner's consent.

Consider that you are currently in a dance with your partner. Your moves affect your partner's moves, so a change on your part should bring about a change in your mate—if you don't use force and you are patient. If you choose the right moves, your mate may not even realize that he or she is changing until the dance is totally different. A seasoned ballroom dancer can gracefully lead his or her partner from the cha-cha to the mambo. By the time the mambo is in full swing, the follower might show a puzzled look that says, *I thought we were doing the cha-cha. What happened to the "chas"?*

Most who work in the field of psychology have heard the story about a woman who rants to her psychiatrist that her husband is a rat. She wants to develop the courage to leave him, so she tells the psychiatrist that she has picked out the date she will go. More than just leave him, the woman confides that she wants to hurt her husband the way he has hurt her. She is determined to follow through.

The psychiatrist tells her that he has a plan that will really knock her husband for a loop when she leaves. He suggests that right up until the day she leaves, she should be especially kind and sweet to the "rat," cooking his favorite meals, acting as if the way he behaves doesn't bother her. Then, when he least suspects it, she should just walk out and have him served with divorce papers. He'll never see it coming, so her vengeance will be a real kick in the teeth.

The woman loved the idea and decided to implement the plan right away. She made an appointment with the psychiatrist to come back a week after her set "D-Day." Several weeks after D-Day, the psychiatrist hadn't heard from her. He called the woman to inquire about her missed appointment. Had the plan worked?

"This is weird," she answered. "By the time I was ready to leave, he had completely changed, so my reasons for leaving him disappeared. I'm actually okay staying with him now. He's better than he has been in a long time. Thanks anyway."

Damned If You Do and Damned If You Don't (also Known as the Schnook or Schmuck Phenomenon)

When I was 18 and my brother was 16, we wore the same size in clothing. One night I had a date with someone I had just met, and when I was figuring out what to wear, I went into my brother's closet in his room and found a beautiful new shirt hanging there. My brother walked in just as I was trying it on. With one arm in the shirt sleeve, I said to him, "Hey, do you mind if I wear this tonight?" Clearly annoyed, he blurted, "Yes, I do mind!" I retorted, "*Excuse me!*" I took the shirt off in a huff, made a show of hanging it back in his closet, and stalked out.

Afterward, my brother couldn't let go of my infraction. He kept arguing with me about what I had done, regardless of how much I told him to back off. Over and over I heard myself saying, "Okay, okay already! That's enough! I put the shirt back. I'm not going to wear it. You happy now?"

No, he was not happy. Nor would he stop expressing his displeasure. Finally, he said what was on his mind in a manner that sank in: "By putting the shirt on without checking with me first—and then only asking me if you could wear it because I walked into the room—you put me in a lose-lose position. If I said, 'Yes,' you were going to wear it anyway, so I hadn't given you anything that you didn't already have. If I said, 'No, put it back,' then I was the obnoxious, bad guy who was too stingy to lend his brother a shirt. Don't you see? You took away any opportunity I could have had to be gracious. I'm either a schnook [someone who gets taken advantage of] or a schmuck [an obnoxious, bad guy]. I don't want to be in either position. They both feel awful."

His words made a big impression on me because I understood the position I had placed him in. I saw that I was using force—either by forcing him to let me wear the shirt that I already had on or by forcing him to make me take it off, after which I could act all huffy at his stinginess.

Giving others a real choice is far more powerful. If you release someone from force, the individual is free to choose.

Imagine if I had changed the scenario with my brother by using a different approach: *Hey, I saw an incredibly great-looking, new shirt in your closet, and I have an outrageous request that you absolutely do not have to agree to unless you want to. I would love it if you'd let me wear the shirt on my date tonight.*

My brother's potential response: *I would, but I haven't even had a chance to wear it myself yet and I want to do that before I lend it out.*

My potential follow-up: *Hey, no problem. I understand. It's a cool shirt. If for some reason you change your mind before I go out, let me know. I'd be happy to dry clean your shirt if I did wear it. But it's fine either way.*

My brother might have relented since the alternative phrasing presents a respectful proposal (not coercion or force) with a win-win conclusion (he would be rewarded with free dry cleaning and gratitude from me for being a great brother; I would look sharp for my date). Even if he said No, the respect I demonstrated would have carried forward to other areas in our relationship.

Keep in mind that we use force when we feel powerless. If you act unilaterally without checking with your partner, your actions will often impact the other in some way. If you acknowledge this and correct it, you will prevent yourself from unwittingly using force. Thus, you will protect the natural desire you and your partner have to please one another.

Some of the couples I have counseled initially respond to this notion with skepticism. *If I ask my partner for a favor, he/she won't agree to it. It's easier for me to do what I want and worry about my partner's reaction later.* That rationale reminds me of an old adage: "It is easier to ask for forgiveness than to get permission." It may be so, but not asking robs your partner of the chance to be generous, loving, and gracious, and you're setting yourself up. Force begets force. Sooner or later, your mate will answer your unilateral move with one of his or her own.

Amazingly, in spite of the unintentional use of force, mutual love plus the desire to please one another is often alive and well (if lying dormant) under the force. By trusting power instead of force, you create an opening for love to appear and surprise you. It feels like a miracle when it happens.

Living with "The Terminator"

Early in my marriage, when my wife, Lauren, and I seemed to spend a good deal of time arguing with each other, I developed a theory that she was actually "the terminator," a cyborg robot sent here from the future with specific programming to "find Jim Goldstein, marry him, and then keep him apart from the things that he loves."

It seemed to me, at that time, that she had fully accomplished her mission because I was, in fact, miserable. I felt that she had successfully discouraged me from pursuing every bit of fun that I used to enjoy before marriage. Instead, she had gotten me to focus on my endless to-do list, to which she added more tasks daily.

As you can see, I felt like a righteous victim at that time in our marriage, and had witnesses and evidence to prove it. The problem with having a theory, any theory, is that the mind tends to organize around it. Pretty soon it starts gathering evidence that supports the theory, conveniently ignoring evidence that disproves it. Since this phenomenon happens regardless of the nature of the theory, it probably behooves us to invent the most charitable theories we can and let our minds produce the appropriate evidence to prove us right.

Gone Fishing

Following my theory about Lauren, it made perfect sense that Lauren seemed to resent my love of fishing; she could always think of reasons why I shouldn't go. Because of her position, I would just sneak out to the river to fish whenever I could. Often, I'd "show up" after the fact hoping she wouldn't question me. I felt justified in being sneaky. Otherwise, how would I ever get to fish? (Of course, I believed she was programmed to thwart that kind of activity!)

As we started to use power instead of force in our relationship, I began revealing the truth, which included my suspicion that she was trying to prevent me from having too much fun in life. I told my truth to her often enough that, over time, I began to get over my suspicion. Eventually, I started noting more and more of her positive qualities.

Transformation

One day, a mind-blowing exchange took place between us. Lauren was looking at my weekly work schedule that I print out for her on Sunday nights.

Casually, she said, "It looks like you have a block of free time on Thursday afternoon. Why don't you take that time off and go fishing?"

I did a quick double take and then stared at her. *WHO ARE YOU and what have you done with my WIFE?* This was the first time I ever heard her suggest that I fish. It marked the beginning of a new theory about my partner.

Shortly after that turning point, I mentioned to Lauren that in all the years that I had been playing and writing music, I had never owned a good piano. I always played on instruments people had given me—if I could "somehow" get it out of their basement. (Those old pianos were real clunkers!) Months later, for my birthday that year, Lauren and her mother conspired to buy me a beautiful six-foot-three-inch Kawai grand piano. She even had to get rid of some of our furniture and rearrange the living room to make room for my new toy. I was so touched by the gift and the trouble my wife had gone to that I didn't know what to say. My terminator theory was no longer operative. She had changed and so had I.

Over the past few years of using *Powerful Partnerships®*, I've developed a new theory about my wife. I believe that she is an angel—sent to me from heaven to make my life happy and joyful as she supports me in the fulfillment of my highest ambitions and desires.

Having collected a tremendous amount of evidence to back up my theory, I am convinced of its validity. Today, when I review my list of adjectives regarding my relationship with my wife, the one item that jumps out at me is the word *blessed*. Blessed has become the truth of my experience. And, angel is a long way from being the terminator.

How to be Powerful

1. Learn to recognize force—whether it is directed towards you or comes from you. Pay attention to your words. Are you subtly using guilt to get your spouse or children to do what you want? *You're not going to make me drive there by myself, are you?* If so, release the recipient of your force. *You know, you don't have to come with me but if you'd like to, I'd love your company on the ride.*

Often force comes across in your tone of voice. Without realizing it, you may be conveying disapproval, annoyance or disdain and thereby blocking your partner's openness to your ideas and desires. Learn to be sensitive to how you feel when your partner speaks. Does what you hear make you want to get closer or move farther away?

Once Lauren said to me, sincerely, "You usually watch TV downstairs or go into your computer room when you could be in here with me. I don't get why you don't want to hang out with me. I would love it if we could talk more." I thought a moment about her observation. It was true. I usually chose to be in a different room in the house when we were both at home. I realized what it was that made me avoid being in the same room. I said, "Here's why I do this. If I spend any time with you alone I anticipate a number of things will happen, all of which make me feel uncomfortable. In the course of our conversation you will either:

1. Ask me to do something I don't particularly want to do.

2. Ask me if I have completed some task that I promised to do.

3. Ask me when I'm going to complete something I have started.

4. Remind me of something that I said I would do and still haven't done yet".

Is it any wonder why I would want to avoid her company? Many of her requests fall into a category in my head called *Things that don't really need to be done now*. They are things that she wants done and wants me to do, part of her to-do list for me. I feel compelled by her logic (forced) to admit that these things are important and I feel obligated to do them since they often require climbing on a ladder or lifting something that she can't lift or contacting someone that she doesn't know (but I do). It's all force in my experience and so I naturally resist her and stay away.

This conversation was very enlightening for Lauren. The dynamic I just described had been going on for years. Since she really did want me to be with her, she started becoming more conscious of the conversations we had when we were together. Over time, I became more comfortable talking with her and worried less about being ambushed with new tasks or interrogations. When I start feeling the old discomfort I just say, "Force," and she backs off.

Reading about this interaction, women might ask, *If you would notice the things around the house that need to be done and do them without being asked, wouldn't that make your wife seem like less of a nag and therefore easier to be with? She wouldn't have to remind you if you would keep your word and do what you promised to do in a timely manner. Aren't you setting her up to be the bad guy by your own irresponsibility/immaturity?*

All of the above may be true but will probably not affect the outcome. As long as I feel force, I'm not likely to change my behavior even if it is pointed out to me that I am being irresponsible and I agree. It would still feel like a "should" to me and thus falls under the "force" category. However, when force is released and replaced by power, all kinds of behaviors are possible that no one could predict from our history together. I may never agree on the necessity of doing the tasks she wants done but I may start doing them because I love her and want to please her and I no longer feel forced.

2. Make a commitment not to use force. When you feel hurt or angry, instead of threatening or attacking the other person, tell the truth. For example, instead of saying, "Just wait until we go to a party at *your* parents' house and I tell everyone how you completely burned three dozen pastries the night of our party," you could say, "I felt embarrassed and stupid at my parents' house when you told everyone about that time I ruined those cabinets while trying to repair them. I felt humiliated when they all laughed." The first statement is fueled by hurt and anger but focuses on threat and retribution in an attempt to get his partner's attention and to control her behavior. The second statement is powerful in that it leaves out the force and emphasizes his experience.

Part of the 10th step of the Alcoholics Anonymous 12-step program states, "…and when we were wrong, promptly admitted it." The same applies to the use of force. When our partner feels force, we need to back off, rephrase our communication or change our tone of voice. If we need to apologize for using force, we should do so as soon as we realize what we were doing.

While on vacation, my wife complained that I was spending too much time at the computer on work related issues. She wanted me to spend more time with her. Though her request was reasonable, I started feeling tremendous added pressure and told her so. "I can't come to the beach until I solve this problem because I have a deadline to meet and I still can't access the Internet to send out these final e-mails to everyone [I was having a technical meltdown with my laptop]. Now I feel doubly guilty because I have to consider what I'm doing to you and our vacation." She came back to me later and said, "I'm sorry. I don't want to add any more pressure to what you are already experiencing. Do what you have to do and come out and see me when you're done. I'll be fine." Her saying that calmed me down and I appreciated her for it. I was able to fix the computer glitch shortly thereafter and we had a nice evening together.

3. Be loving. You may not always feel love for your partner but you can commit to be loving. Do and say the things that you first did and said when your relationship began. By continuing to appreciate your partner and doing kind things for him or her, you become more powerful than you could imagine. Loving acts and words do more to heal a relationship than becoming proficient at expressing yourself in an argument. Figure out what your partner considers loving acts and kind words. Do and say them repeatedly.

For instance, no matter how early it is or how hurried I am, I always kiss my sleeping wife gently on the lips before leaving our bedroom in the morning for work. In response, she smiles as I whisper, "I love you." I know she likes my gesture. Moreover, being loving puts me in touch with how much I love her. As I tell her I love her, the words are true for me. It is not just a perfunctory gesture. I know that being loving is something I can always achieve if I want to, and it does a lot to alleviate any concerns I might have had about losing that loving feeling.

4. Focus on where you want to go, not where you've been. There is something compelling and attractive about a vision. If you focus on and speak about how you want the relationship to be and feel instead of complaining about where it is and where it has been you will move into that vision, start feeling much better and will probably enroll your partner in going there with you. The rule in learning to ride a motorcycle is: *Where you look is where you go.* The bike follows your head movements. There is another saying that cyclists use which is equally valid: *Look where you want to go, not where you want to crash.* These expressions apply to relationships as well. Where you are heading is much more important than anything else in determining your future.

5. Practice telling the truth, the whole truth, and nothing but the truth (especially when you are upset). The *Powerful Partnerships*® program will teach you exactly how to do this.

6. Repair the old glitches (returning to the places where things initially broke down) by telling the truth now about how you felt back then. *Powerful Partnerships*® reveals a unique process called The Four-Channel Clearing™ (coming soon) that will allow you to express yourself completely with nothing truthful left unsaid. It leaves you feeling complete and at peace. You can use it to talk about and heal the oldest upsets that never got resolved.

Power is strength often masquerading as weakness.

CHAPTER 3

Love Never Requires Sacrifice

What you will learn from this chapter:

How to stay true to yourself while pleasing others

One of the underlying principles of *Powerful Partnerships*® is that love—not fear, guilt or manipulation—is the only legitimate motivator in a relationship. Any other motivation would be classified as force. When we act out of love, we feel good doing it; the action becomes its own reward. Giving is done without expectation of a *quid pro quo*. We aren't just "giving to get." When we give out of love, we often have the experience St. Francis described when he wrote, "It is in the giving that we receive."

Imagine how great it would feel if you knew that everything your partner did for you was done out of love, and there was no expectation of future payback, no obligation to return the favor, no score being kept. That is one of the joys of being in a powerful partnership.

Doesn't Love Require Us to Sacrifice Sometimes?

The question of whether or not love requires sacrifice depends on your definition. Many times, we do things for the sake of our relationship that we wouldn't do if we didn't have to consider the other person. Parents may sacrifice going out to dinner or continuing a membership at a club so that they can afford tuition for their child's school. That act is not necessarily sacrifice as I am describing it.

Sacrifice has to do with an experience or a feeling rather than any particular behavior. If the parents eliminate enjoyed activities out of their love and commitment to their children's growth and development, they won't have the experience of sacrifice. If, on the other hand, they resent not being able to go to dinner or to socialize at a club, then the same behavior is a sacrifice; there will be negative consequences for everyone.

How does Powerful Partnerships® describe sacrifice?

By sacrifice, I mean doing something that you don't want to do because you feel obligated in some way. It means saying, "Yes," "Fine," "Okay" or "No Problem" when you really don't mean it. People often acquiesce to requests because they think they should. They'd feel guilty otherwise. That would mean force is in the picture.

What happens when a person does something for the wrong reasons—when he or she feels forced or obligated in some way to do it? As you'll soon see, there is usually hell to pay.

No Good Deed Goes Unpunished

"No good deed goes unpunished" refers to a peculiar phenomenon experienced when an attempt to do something nice for someone backfires. Instead of being thanked for this kindness (good deed), we are not only unappreciated, but we are also blamed or made wrong by the one person we were trying to help. Though it doesn't always happen, there are many instances in which it does. Here are a few.

During the Cold War, Americans gave millions of dollars in foreign aid and technology to Finland only to find out that the Fins were selling US secrets to the Soviets. Americans felt punished for their generosity.

On more than one occasion, a doctor has witnessed a terrible accident. Despite rushing to the injured person's aid at the scene, the professional was later sued by the family of the injured party for not doing enough or for performing a risky procedure.

I remember, many years ago, playing in a rock band at a huge music festival. The members of my group and I were all hungry one afternoon but couldn't leave to get food. Since we could be asked to go on stage at any moment, we had to be ready and available at all times. A band member's girlfriend volunteered to go to the concession stand for us. We each gave her our order and waited for her return. After about 90 minutes, as we were wondering what happened to her, she finally returned, exhausted from standing in line.

She had a huge box of food, but as with most rock concerts back then, the concession stands were ill-equipped to handle huge crowds, and many of the items we ordered were no longer in stock. I remember her handing a carton to me saying, "Here, Jimmy, they were out of turkey sandwiches, so I got you a yogurt. You owe me $2.50." I remember responding sarcastically, "Thanks a lot, Sue. I'm allergic to dairy." Most of the other hungry band members weren't particularly grateful either, since none of them got what they ordered and were still expected to pay.

You can imagine how Sue felt. Though she had tried to do her best after standing in line in the hot sun, Sue was not only unappreciated, but she was criticized for her arbitrary food choices. I can guess what she was thinking. *This is what I get for trying to be nice. Never again! They can all starve for all I care!* No good deed goes unpunished.

Sacrifice: No Good Deed Goes Unpunished—Twice!

Sacrifice in relationships is particularly insidious in that the good deed *always yields two punishments:* First, when we punish ourselves for acting in conflict with our own integrity (for not being true to ourselves). Second, when we punish the person for whom we sacrificed.

It's important to remember that we don't purposely punish the other person or ourselves. We unwittingly and often unconsciously set things in motion so that the punishment is only apparent later. It's not until the experience of punishment shows up that we realize that either we or our partner must have sacrificed.

Consider the following true scenario:

> Rick: "Will you come with me to my company Christmas Party?"
>
> Diane: "I really don't want to go. I went last year and I hated it. I didn't know anyone there."

Rick: "It will be awkward to be there by myself. Everyone will be asking about you. C'mon, go with me."

Diane: "Please don't make me go. I find these affairs deadly dull."

Rick: "I went with you to your high school reunion and I didn't know anyone there either, remember?"

Diane: (Thinks a minute) "Yeah, you did. Okay, I'll go."

This last statement is a sacrifice on Diane's part, even though she may not realize it. She has now agreed to go to the party out of a sense of fairness and obligation; Rick did attend her high school reunion. He may have won the battle here, but you will see how he will lose the war.

Later at the party, Rick and Diane approach the buffet table.

Diane: "I can't eat anything on this buffet."

Rick: "Why not?"

Diane: "I'm allergic to shrimp. I don't eat red meat. You know I can't stand broccoli, and the salad has bacon bits in it. Fine! I'll just have bread."

Love Never Requires Sacrifice

Both have felt the consequences of sacrifice. Diane is punished because she will not be able to eat anything. Rick is punished because he is accompanied by a hungry, dissatisfied wife who will be unhappy every moment she is there. She will give him looks all night as if to say, *Can we go now?* Neither will enjoy the event, and if they dissected their problem, they would trace the cause of their suffering back to sacrifice.

Beware the Double Whammy

Sacrifice is a real relationship wrecker. Consider this cruel fact: You are punished not only if you sacrifice, but also if you allow your partner to sacrifice for you. Therefore, to avoid punishment, it is important that you not only be true to yourself, but that you also *not allow sacrifice on your behalf.*

Suppose a husband pressures his wife to have sex. She consents but not because she wants to please him or is interested in sex. She may comply to get him to stop asking or to ease her guilt over having gone this long without having sex with him or because she is afraid he might find someone else if she doesn't yield to his demands.

What is the likely double punishment from that type of sacrifice? It may be mild if, for instance, neither of them enjoy it much and, therefore, feel less close to each other than before the sex. Or it may be harsh for both parties if, for instance, shortly after having sex, the woman develops a urinary tract infection which is painful (her punishment) and prevents them from having sex for quite a while (his punishment).

One time, early in our relationship, I said to Lauren, "Would you make dinner?" I still remember her reaction. She hesitated a little before saying, "Okay," as her eyelids sort of half-closed wearily and then reopened. I later realized that this was a telling (albeit unconscious) sign of sacrifice on her part.

After that, everything seemed fine. She started cooking a nice casserole and looked like she was really into it. She placed the meal, which smelled and looked delicious, in front of me. I took a bite and then quickly spit it out. I said, "This has cumin in it. I hate cumin!"

> She looked horrified. "I thought it was turmeric you couldn't stand."

> "I like turmeric fine", I said. "It's cumin I can't stand."

Needless to say, we were both punished at that point. She had put a lot of time and effort into making something for me that I wasn't going to eat. That was her punishment. My punishment was that, as hungry as I was, I was not going to be able to eat what was just prepared for me.

I am now acutely attuned to Lauren's indications of sacrifice, and she knows when I am about to sacrifice as well. If I ever see her eyelids dip to half-mast, I say, "Hey, you don't have to cook (go on that errand with me, pick up my book at the library, etc.). We can go out to dinner." I only want her to do what she does out of love. No force, no obligation, no *quid pro quo*, no guilt. Just love. I don't want her to punish herself or me.

Beyond sacrifice, I make sure that Lauren feels no obligation to cook for me. Neither of us particularly likes to cook. She does many of the things around the house because she wants to and because she loves me. I love everything she cooks partly because I see her cooking for me as an act of love. If she felt obligated to make dinner, it would change everything.

How Can Sacrifice Be Eliminated from a Relationship?

First, promise each other that you will not knowingly sacrifice for one another. Promise, also, that you won't allow your partner to sacrifice on your behalf. Give each other permission to identify a sacrifice whenever it occurs. Promise to release the sacrificing party from his or her obligation and talk about it. Perhaps a compromise can be reached that eliminates the sacrificial portion of the activity. Talking usually helps.

Consider the following two scenarios:

> Sarah: (After a nice dinner at a restaurant) "Will you stop by the mall with me before we go home? I need to get a dress for the party."
>
> Eric: "Not without sacrificing."
>
> Sarah: "Okay. I'll see if I can get my mom to go with me tomorrow."
>
> In the previous instance, they both avoided punishments arising from Eric's sacrifice. Let's see another way to address the situation:
>
> Sarah: Do you think you could go with me and not have it be a sacrifice?"
>
> Eric: "Possibly. Maybe I could stop in the bookstore for a paperback first so that I have something to do at the mall. I just don't want to be bored. If you don't mind me just reading while you try stuff on, it wouldn't feel like a sacrifice.

Sometimes just announcing that you are sacrificing and seeing that your partner is willing to release you from having to do it is enough to transform the experience of sacrifice. At that point, it can be fine to proceed. Remember: Self expression is healing.

What If You Don't Realize You Are Sacrificing Until Later?

This is quite common. Your partner asks you to do something that, at first, you don't think you would mind doing. Then, halfway through the activity, you realize that it isn't what you want to be doing at all. If you have already made an agreement with each other not to sacrifice, then all you need to do is say, "I know I said I'd go with you, but this is starting to feel like a sacrifice." Sometimes, just admitting how you feel is enough to change it. Having identified the sacrifice, you no longer feel like you are sacrificing. In the end, if neither you nor your partner is punished, neither has sacrificed.

Can You Be in a Committed Relationship and Not Do Anything You Don't Want to Do?

I once tested the limits of not sacrificing. Our children were both around six months old, and they woke up frequently in the middle of the night. As soon as we got one of them back to sleep, the other would wake up, start crying, and reawaken the first one. We were losing our minds from lack of sleep.

During this time frame, I was developing my theory about sacrifice. I remember lying in bed at 3:00 in the morning, listening to my son wailing in the next room. I asked myself, "Do I really want to get up again, change his diaper, and do whatever I have to do to get him back to sleep?" The answer was a resounding *No!*

I considered the situation and decided that if I rose from my bed again, it would be a sacrifice. Therefore, if my theory was correct, I was liable to punish myself and my son for sacrificing. As a result, I decided not to get up.

But my son continued to wail. Finally, it hit me that I created this situation. I asked for my kids, I wanted them, I helped create them, and they were dependent on Lauren and me for their needs. Right then, something changed inside of me. Getting up no longer felt like a sacrifice. Instead, it felt like a commitment. I got up, changed his diaper, put him back in the crib, and he fell asleep instantly. I stumbled back to bed and I fell asleep instantly. The next morning, I woke up refreshed. No punishment. No sacrifice. Neat!

Rules and Consciousness

Often, an inverse relationship exists between rules and consciousness. The more conscious and aware we are, the less we need rules of behavior; the more we follow the rules, the less conscious we can become. Neither rules nor consciousness is preferable or more important than the other. Both are vital to living in society.

For example, if we were all conscious of where we were driving, each of us would stay on the right side of the road, especially around curves, to avoid oncoming traffic. Therefore, we wouldn't need lines painted on the highway (rules) to keep us from zigzagging or passing other cars too closely. Yet without lines we would have to spend an excessive amount of energy being conscious of our proximity to other cars and determining whether it is safe to pass. The lines relieve us of having to be acutely conscious of where we are every second. We are able to drive comfortably by simply obeying the rules.

Conversely, if we just followed the rules without any consciousness, we could end up passing a car when we shouldn't. Don't the dotted lines permit this? They do, but blindly abiding by the rule disregards important considerations, such as current road conditions (wet or icy) and visual constraints (glaring sun) that might make the maneuver unsafe.

What follows is an example of a couple who made promises to each other and established rules regarding the distribution of house duties that seemed reasonable at first. Nevertheless, without love or consciousness behind them, these rules broke down into *shoulds, musts* and other forms of force and sacrifice.

Pam and Alan thought of a way to divide kitchen duties. They agreed that whoever cooked wouldn't have to clean up afterwards. Many couples have hit on this idea and have found that assigning cooking to one and cleaning to another works beautifully, especially if one hates to clean and the other hates to cook. Pam and Alan agreed to take turns since each liked to cook.

For a while, their arrangement worked pretty well. Over time, however, the one cooking tended to become more creative and expansive in the kitchen, using many more pots than if he or she had clean-up duty. The person who had to clean up was treated to a lovely meal, but felt forced to deal with a big messy kitchen.

Sometimes, when Alan came home to an elaborate dinner that Pam was all excited about having prepared, he'd say, "Gee I'm not really hungry tonight. I was hoping that we could just have a salad."

What happened here? Without consciousness, mere adherence to rules can disconnect us from our desire to consider the effects of our behavior on others as well as from what we would do out of love.

The solution to Pam and Alan's problem was a re-examination of their agreement from the standpoint of *sacrifice*. In this case, what started out as a good idea became a sacrifice; therefore, they needed to reassess until a win-win answer was found.

CHAPTER **4**

How To Determine What Is True

What you will learn from this chapter:

How to identify your truth and everyone else's

How to Tell the Truth

Powerful Partnerships® defines truth in a unique way. My focus will be on the truth of your experience, what is personally, subjectively true for you. The truth is anything that you say that can't be debated, argued with, or overturned by anyone—ever. The truth, therefore, is incontrovertible and irrefutable. Note: This is not *the* Truth (with a capital T), such as *Buddha's Four Noble Truths*, the central teachings of Buddhism. In this application, we are interested in the truth of **your experience.**

The utterance of this truth has healing powers of its own.

To establish how your words can become the irrefutable truth, consider the following statement: *Your sister looks beautiful.* Does it pass the truth test? The answer is, *No.* The reason is that someone, somewhere, could debate it. Consequently, phrased in that way, the statement cannot be true. Ten thousand people could agree that she looks beautiful, but that does not make our statement true. However, *I love how your sister looks* would be true by my definition. No one anywhere can debate me on that last statement.

Determining What Is True

Keep in mind that the truth, as I have defined it, doesn't engender argument, debate, or rebuttal. Upon hearing your truth, the listener will be unable to disagree with you. The listener may think that you are absurd, but he or she can't controvert what you just said because it was true for you. If, according to our standard, the other person can take issue with what you said, then you weren't telling the irrefutable truth.

In conversation, people say all sorts of things that obscure the truth. This is partly because they don't always know what is true for them. Often, individuals are uncomfortable being outspoken, so they carefully phrase their words. In any event, if you listen to what people say, you will be able to discern what is true and what isn't simply by answering this question: *Could I—or anyone else on the planet—disagree with what I just heard?* If so, then the person is not telling the irrefutable truth. Perhaps they are telling their opinion or suspicion or belief as if it is true. But that is not their truth. Remember, if you or anyone else can debate what they just said, it wasn't true by my *Powerful Partnerships*® definition.

People often frame untrue statements as if they are true. Consider this one: *The truth is you said that just for spite!* Though the impassioned accusation is spoken with conviction, it is not true within the framework of *Powerful Partnerships*® because the statement is debatable. The listener could disagree, so the expression is merely a suspicion or a belief.

Applying *Powerful Partnerships*®' straightforward definition to anything you hear reveals that few people speak the truth. More often than not, people state their strongly held opinions and beliefs as if they are true.

The Truth Test

Examine the following statements in light of the irrefutable truth. Are any of them true? Apply the test: *Could anyone anywhere on the planet disagree?* If the answer is Yes, then the statement cannot be true. If the statement is not true, contemplate what the truth might be in each case. You can check your thoughts with mine at the end.

- *I didn't say anything because I knew how you would react.*

- *You always leave your coat on that chair.*

- *I need you to help me look up those phone numbers.*

- *I would really appreciate it if you would knock before entering my office.*

- *I resent your self-righteous attitude.*

- *You know that irritates me.*

- *How long do you think it's been since we had heat in this building?*

- *I haven't stopped doing these log entries since you left for lunch.*

- *Who do you think is supposed to clean up those dishes that you left in the sink?*

- *After this, are you going to help me with the filing?*

- *We're both so immature sometimes.*

- *I knew that would happen.*

- *I know you say that you'll practice this stuff but you won't do it.*

- *He never listens to me.*
- *I always clean up after myself.*
- *I feel that you're trying to control the situation.*
- *You're just too proud to admit you're wrong.*
- *Who left the soda can on the conference table?*
- *Do you have to take off tomorrow?*
- *You don't need that much sugar in your coffee.*
- *Why are you watching that show? You've already seen it.*

For each example, I'll offer my interpretation of the truth behind the words:

I didn't say anything because I knew how you would react.
How could anyone know how someone else would react?

My interpretation of the truth: *I didn't say anything because I was afraid you'd react like you did in the past.*

You always leave your coat on that chair. Does anyone always do anything?

My interpretation of the truth: *I don't like to see your coat on that chair. I want you to hang it up when you come in.*

I need you to help me look up those phone numbers. Needs are debatable.

My interpretation of the truth: *I'd like you to help me look up those numbers. Will you?*

I would really appreciate it if you would knock before entering my office. This feels like resentment cloaked in an appreciation.

My interpretation of the truth: *I don't like it when you enter without knocking. Sometimes it startles me. I want you to knock and wait for me to say 'come in' before entering my office.*

I resent your self-righteous attitude. The reference is vague.

My interpretation of the truth: *I feel like I'm being criticized by someone who doesn't believe he makes any mistakes and I don't like it.*

You know that irritates me. No one knows exactly what another person knows nor can anyone always accurately assess another's motives.

My interpretation of the truth: *Please don't do that. I told you before that it irritates me and it still does.*

How long do you think it's been since we had heat in this building? This may not just be an innocent inquiry.

My interpretation of the truth: *It really bothers me that we have been without heat this long.*

I haven't stopped doing these log entries since you left for lunch. This does not sound like a simple telegraphing of information.

My interpretation of the truth: *This log entry job has been a total pain. I'd like to be appreciated for how long and tedious this job is and for how diligently I have been working on it. Also, a large raise and the rest of the day off would certainly make my day if you could swing it.*

Who do you think is supposed to clean up those dishes that you left in the sink? This is not really a question.

My interpretation of the truth: I *don't like seeing those dishes in the sink. I want you to clean your own dishes.*

After this are you going to help me with the filing? This isn't a question; it's a request.

My interpretation of the truth: *I would like you to help me with the filing after this. Would you, please?*

We're both so immature sometimes. The word *both* makes this untrue. A person might easily respond to this with, *Speak for yourself!*

My interpretation of the truth: *Sometimes I see my behavior as immature. I'd like you to say that you behave immaturely at times yourself. You don't have to, of course, but I'd like it if you did.*

I knew that would happen.
No one knows the future.

My interpretation of the truth: *I was afraid that might happen.*

I know you say that you'll practice this stuff but you won't do it. This is a prediction about the future.

My interpretation of the truth: *I'm afraid you won't practice this stuff even though you say you will.*

He never listens to me.
Never is debatable.

My interpretation of the truth: *Much of the time, I don't feel listened to.*

I always clean up after myself.
Like the word, never, *always* elicits a challenge as to its veracity.

My interpretation of the truth: *I believe that I clean up after myself most of the time and I want you to do that, too.*

I feel that you're trying to control the situation. *I feel that you* is not a true feeling.

My interpretation of the truth: *I am starting to feel controlled.*

You're just too proud to admit you're wrong. This is one person's uncharitable assessment of another's character.

My interpretation of the truth: *When you are wrong, I want you to admit it.*

Who left the soda can on the conference table? This doesn't sound like an innocent inquiry.

My interpretation of the truth: *I brought guests into the conference room and there was an empty soda can on the table. I felt embarrassed and later, angry. I want you guys to keep this room immaculate. If you eat in here, leave no evidence that you did.*

Do you have to take off tomorrow?
This feels more like a plaintive, guilt-producing whine than a question.

My interpretation of the truth: *I feel completely swamped. If there is a way that you could reschedule your day off tomorrow and help me finish this, I'd be grateful.*

You don't need that much sugar in your coffee. Telling another what they need and don't need will often engender a defensive response.

My interpretation of the truth: *I'm afraid you will get fat (or give yourself a sugar high) from eating that much sugar. I want you to use less.*

Why are you watching that show? You've already seen it. Beware of "why" questions, which tend to hide truthful statements.

My interpretation of the truth: *I don't want you to watch that rerun. I want you to turn off the TV and pay attention to me. I want you to find listening and talking to me much more interesting than anything you could watch on TV.*

Just the Facts

The truth is based on fact. A fact is an objective and verifiable observation. It is either occurring now, or it happened in the past. In relationships, it is often something that was said or done or something that transpired.

For example, even though you might know how to discern a condescending attitude, stating that a person was patronizing would not be a fact according to our definition. Therefore, be aware of the difference between fact and inference. No one could dispute a fact, but an inference is subject to interpretation.

An attitude is made up of particular words, tone of voice, gestures and mannerisms, all of which could be observed and imitated, and, thus, are the facts underlying the assessment. Healing takes place by identifying and referring to the facts rather than assuming that your interpretations are true.

Refining Truthful Statements

Consider the following examples of how you can turn an assumption into a factual statement.

> **Assertion:** *I just can't take your irresponsible, passive-aggressive behavior.*

Truth: *You said you were going to call me back in two minutes. I waited 30 minutes in that guy's office and the phone never rang and I didn't like that.*

Or: *I was standing for 30 minutes in that guy's office waiting for the phone to ring. I felt frustrated and awkward and embarrassed.*

Both truthful statements contain several facts—events *(phone never rang)* and actions *(I waited)* that occurred as well as words *(I don't like)* that described how the person felt about the situation.

While the statements above are true, they don't represent the *whole truth.* Although you would be off to a good start, you won't necessarily resolve your upset feelings or bring yourself to a complete state of forgiveness if you stopped there. The Four-Channel Clearing™, to be addressed later, demonstrates how to tell the truth, the whole truth, and nothing but the truth in a manner that totally transforms your mood, attitude, and even your opinion of the other person.

The Truth Leaves Us Speechless

Here's another interesting observation: While in the presence of a person who tells the truth, you will find that your mind becomes quiet. Instead of the usual chatter that starts to crank in your head when another is talking, your mind is free to relax rather than work on a comment or rebuttal in response.

I have observed people as they are hearing the truth. Often, they get a strange look on their face. My interpretation of that look is: *I can't do anything with what you just said.*

If you catch yourself thinking about what you will say as soon as the other person's lips stop moving, the individual is not telling you the irrefutable truth. If it is the truth, your mind can't get a firm purchase on a comeback or rebuttal. At least momentarily, you will be speechless. When you finally do speak, you will tend to say something that is true for you in response to the prior truth.

"Why" Questions Often Mask the Truth

When a person asks *why*, it may be an innocent inquiry—someone may be wondering why something is so. For example, I might ask: *Why do the lamps in this room have 50-watt bulbs while the lamps in the other rooms have 60-watt bulbs?* If I'm curious, my tone must sound neutral or innocent; otherwise, you might suspect some other truth lurks beneath the thoughts I haven't shared.

In contrast, I might ask a different question with a tone of annoyance: *Why didn't you say so before?*

Frankly, I don't want to know *why*. I am asking *why* instead of making a true statement. My true statement might be this: *I don't like finding this out now. I would have wanted you to tell me this as soon as you knew.*

With that insight, be wary of answering why questions unless you are convinced of the neutrality or innocence of the statement. How might you respond? *I don't like answering **why** questions. If you've got something to say, please make a statement and I'll be glad to listen.*

---

*Be wary of answering **why** questions unless you are convinced of the neutrality or innocence of the statement*

The Truth, the Whole Truth, and Nothing But the Truth

Have you ever wondered why, when a person is sworn in at a courtroom, we make the individual swear to tell not only the truth, but also the whole truth and nothing but the truth? There is a good reason. It is quite possible to tell the truth and not tell the whole truth.

A mom confronts her son about fighting with his younger brother. He protests, "I didn't punch him!"

He omits that he slapped his sibling in the face. The second fact belies his original statement. The example highlights the importance of continuing your process until the whole truth is expressed if healing is your goal. When we cover The Four-Channel Clearing™, you will learn how to express and reveal the complete irrefutable truth.

Likewise, you might say something that is true, yet mix it with something that is untrue—such as your opinion or belief. Your words, then, will not have the desired healing effect. You will, in fact, open the door for the person listening to debate with you.

Telling the truth all the time might seem boring. Isn't there more to life than your feelings about the facts? Opinions, assertions, beliefs, theories, stories, suspicions, or interpretations are usually much more interesting! Usually I love to listen to the political talk shows on Sunday morning network television. Not much truth (as I have defined it) is spoken, yet I find the rhetoric to be stimulating and thought-provoking.

There is nothing wrong with having a point of view and stating it—unless you are upset. Then, it's extremely important for you to stick to the truth i.e., how you feel about the facts.

If you stray from the truth when you are upset, you risk aggravating the other person and engendering an argument that escalates. Your opinion will spark the other's opinion; your theory will invite the other's theory. Soon, you're off to the races.

Sticking Your Arms out the Window

Imagine that you are riding in fast-moving, old-fashioned train on a beautiful day—the kind where you can open the windows. It makes sense to keep your arms inside the train, doesn't it? Sticking your arm out the window may not always cause harm, but there's a chance that you could get it whacked by a tree branch or some other obstacle whizzing by. That's how it is with telling the truth. If you squeeze in an opinion or two, it's like sticking your arm out the window of the train. Maybe nothing will happen. Maybe you can get your arm back in before it hits a tree branch. Likewise, maybe you can start telling the truth again before the listener reacts to your opinion or belief. It's risky and sometimes dangerous to mix it up, though. Stick to the truth until you have said it all. Keep your arms inside the train until you reach your destination, just in case.

CHAPTER **5**

Intimacy and Boundaries

What you will learn from this chapter:

How to have an intimate relationship by respecting your boundaries and everyone else's

What Is Intimacy?

Intimacy is not just getting close to someone. As Virginia Satir, a famous family therapist, once said, "Intimacy is about spaces, knowing when to step back and when it is alright to move into a space."

Did you ever meet someone who firmly believed that everyone needed and deserved a hug every day? The person who feels this way often gives you a hug whether you want one or not. How does it feel when you are hugged by someone who just assumes you'd like it? Does it make you feel closer to that person? Are you more intimate afterwards, than you were before the hug? I don't think so.

In order to be intimate with someone, you need to know who you are and who the other person is. Yet how can you know this without learning something about the individual? Not everyone likes to be hugged, but some people love it. The way you learn about and respect another person is by discovering his or her boundaries and teaching the individual about yours.

Whenever someone talks about the incredible relationship he or she has with a new girlfriend or boyfriend, my first thought is *Have you had any fights yet*? Couples who get along great and feel terrific about each other are not necessarily intimate. Until they hit a glitch, rub each other the wrong way, inadvertently hurt each other's feelings, and get over what is upsetting them, their intimate relationship remains untested.

I knew of two families who had known each other for years, even celebrating Thanksgiving together; they felt like relatives. After many years, however, something happened. One family did not show up after they were invited to the other family's daughter's wedding. The family giving the wedding, hurt and flabbergasted that their best friends had something more important to do than be part of their daughter's wedding, never said anything.

Despite being friends without a single disagreement in all of those years, the family who gave the wedding had some reason why they couldn't make it to the upcoming combined Thanksgiving dinner. The excuse sounded legitimate, but even so, it marked the beginning of the end of this long relationship.

> *People need to understand and respect each other's sensitivities (their boundaries) in order to achieve intimacy with each other.*

Crossing the Line

We all have an invisible, flexible boundary around our body. When someone violates that boundary, we start to feel uncomfortable. Despite what we might believe about how open we think we are, this boundary is what it is—it can't be faked. When someone moves into our space, we either back away (physically) to restore our boundary or we express ourselves in some way to let the intruder know that he or she has crossed a line and should back up.

In addition to physical boundaries, we all have emotional boundaries, areas where conversation is not welcome. If someone crosses the line with your emotions, you might feel just as uncomfortable as if a physical boundary were broken. You've probably heard at least one person say, "I can't believe she just asked me that question!" The individual is shocked that another would violate an emotional boundary.

Commonly, people have no idea that their words will violate another's boundaries. They utter insensitive remarks without realizing what they say might be taken as hurtful. For instance, many adoptive parents have told me about individuals asking, "Who is the child's *real* mother?"

At times, the only appropriate response is to adopt a line of reasoning known as Hanlon's Razor: "Never ascribe to malice that which is adequately explained by stupidity."

Since some people commonly yet inadvertently violate boundaries, it's important to express yourself to let others know where your boundaries are and when they've been crossed. Your willingness to be truthful when your boundaries have been violated allows others to demonstrate that they can respect you and your sensitivities. If you merely avoid someone after a violation, the individual will never learn how to navigate your "coastline" correctly.

Intimacy and Forgiveness

The problem with couples who never fight is that they tend to drift apart over time. They may have had a disagreement earlier in their relationship that left each partner feeling uncomfortable; thereafter, they made a tacit agreement never to disagree again. This is called *confluence.* Studies which compare couples who last and those who don't have shown that one of the determining factors is whether or not they have disagreements and work through them. Interestingly, the couples who never argue are the ones most likely to end in divorce. It's not the fact that couples argue that makes for a longer lasting relationship, but the difference lies in their ability to argue and get through to the other side of the argument to forgiveness.

If each of your arguments allows you to know yourself and your partner a little better by learning what bothers each of you, then this is a good thing. Gaining such insights about your partner gives you a chance to show your respect and love by how you behave thereafter. As we said earlier, intimacy, in the end, is based on a series of "forgivenesses." With each episode of forgiveness, you get a little closer by accepting yourself and the other person a little more. Part of the way you express your love is by learning where all the "buttons" are on your partner— *and not pushing them.*

CHAPTER **6**

Modeling Children's Behavior

What you will learn from this chapter:

How to be powerful by becoming more childlike without behaving childishly

A good deal of the inspiration for *Powerful Partnerships*® came from my observations of young children, especially my own. There is a magical age between two and five years when children speak their irrefutable truth almost exclusively. They tell you clearly what they like, what they don't like, how they feel, and what they want. At this point in their lives, they are immensely powerful beings. Adults tend to give them most of what they want because children never use force—only self-expression.

When my children were young, they often asked for the most outrageous things. More often than not, I found myself trying to accommodate them. If I could, I would do what they asked because I wanted to make them happy. I never felt forced to do anything for them.

Later, as they learned force from me and other adults, they became less powerful.

When my daughter was at that magically powerful age, she loved to ask, "Dad, could we have ice cream?" Often, we had finished dessert a half-hour before. I would usually refuse, explaining that we had already eaten our dessert at the dinner table. She would continue to ask over and over again, each time sounding like it was the first time she ever made that request. I never felt forced to give it to her. I typically said, "Thea, you've asked me this 20 times, and each time I've told you 'No.'" She then would say, "I know, Dad... but can we?" She would use the same innocent tone of voice—as if she were merely curious whether this time I might have changed my mind. I found it exasperating but somehow endearing because Thea was utterly guileless in her request. Most often, I replied, "Alright, you can but just one scoop for you and one for your brother. And don't spill any!" She would say, "Thanks, Dad," without the slightest indication that she knew she had worn me down or manipulated me. In the end, I never felt abused by her asking. I was impressed by her tenacity, actually. It was all pretty amazing.

Later, as she learned how adults talked, she would make requests more than once for something I had denied her. However, her asking would be followed by an admonition like. "Dad, you promised!" Or, "You let Todd do it!" (Now I must do the same for her!)

Her exclamation evoked guilt in me. She was right. Regarding the promise, I *had to* do as she wished, yet I noticed that I didn't *feel* like doing what she wanted anymore. She was beginning to use force; as a result, she was also losing her power. Our negotiations weren't as much fun after that.

It's not that people shouldn't keep their word and be held to their promises or attempt to be fair. Nevertheless, when the motivation for action is fear or guilt, or the feeling that one *should* do something, the desire to want to please the other person diminishes. Love, again, is the only legitimate motivator.

The Healing Effects of Self-Expression

When not suppressed by adults, children fully let themselves feel angry or hurt. In doing so, they quickly get over whatever is bothering them. Their reaction to disappointments often seems extreme and overblown, yet the behavior works for them. Before their tears are dry, they are happy again with no aftereffects from the incident. Forgiveness and healing follow naturally from full self-expression.

Sneezing

Doesn't a sneeze seem like an overreaction to getting a little dust in your nose? It's loud and messy. Sometimes your whole body gets involved. Yet, it works. Sneezing blows out the dust or gets rid of the tickle. And don't you feel better afterward! Besides, as loud as it can be, sneezing is pretty acceptable. People tend to allow us whatever room we need for that type of self-expression without much criticism or shame. They even bless us after we sneeze, hoping that we're not catching a cold.

As in the case of sneezing, self-expression often requires letting off steam, allowing uncomfortable feelings to come to the surface, saying things that seem over the top. Despite all of that, when done without force, each of those conditions can be tremendously healing.

Up with Petty!

You might have suppressed your self-expression for fear that your complaints or wishes might seem petty. Children have no such problem. My daughter, looking at the food on her dinner plate, used to exclaim, "I can't eat those peas! They're touching the potatoes!" I'd offer to wash them off but that wouldn't help. They had already touched the potatoes and were, therefore, irreparably damaged. Though petty and irrational, the condition was true for her. She didn't like the peas or want them if they had touched the potatoes. Did I have to serve her a new plate with untouched peas? Of course, not. But at least she got to express herself and thereby got over what was bothering her.

As adults, we make excuses for our desires or annoyances so that we can't be accused of being petty. But sometimes the littlest things are what most upset us. If we can't talk about them honestly, how can we get over them? By shaming ourselves out of our feelings? No! So I say *up with petty*!

Let yourself be petty on the way to getting over what bothers you. You'll heal more quickly than if you suppressed your feelings to hide your pettiness. For example, rather than insisting that Philadelphia® cream cheese tastes better than the store brand, which costs half as much, just say, *I know this might sound petty, and I can't justify my preference with good reasons, but I want to eat only Philadelphia® brand. Even if I failed a blindfolded taste test between the two, I'd still want Philadelphia® Okay?*

Making a Big Deal Out of Nothing

Have you noticed that when you are upset about something, if a person says, *I think you're making a big deal out of nothing*, you will definitely not be *less* upset? If anything, those words will have the opposite effect. In fact, you might protest: *It's not nothing! It is a big deal!*

No one can talk you out of being petty by telling you that you are being petty or ridiculous. It doesn't matter that someone else says the issue should or should not bother you. Rather than allowing ourselves to be talked out of our feelings, we would do better just expressing them to get over them—even if they are petty and we are super-sensitive.

Dan and Cindy often had arguments over the care and feeding of their pets. Dan was always worried about something bad happening to the cats and insisted on all kinds of precautions to protect them from harm. Dan warned Cindy not to leave the cabinet doors open; one of the cats might crawl inside and accidentally poison herself on some household chemical. Cindy, who had owned cats all her life without incident, thought Dan's concerns were ridiculous. She tried to tell him that he was being overly protective and making a big deal out of nothing. This never helped. Dan would dig in with a logical argument to defend his position. He presented examples of animals that had died because such precautions weren't used. Dan and Cindy, quite entrenched in their positions, each gathered more witnesses and evidence to prove their theories about what is best for animals.

Dan would have garnered Cindy's cooperation more effectively if he had not tried to bolster his position logically. He just wanted her to close the cabinet doors. Cindy might have closed them as a gesture of love if she did not have to agree with the validity of his argument. Instead, by asserting that he was making a big deal over nothing, Cindy inflamed Dan and a resolution became less likely.

Still Children after All these Years

In some ways, adults remain emotionally like children. They have been taught (through guilt, shame, anger, and other types of force) to deny and suppress their feelings so as not to seem petty, selfish, demanding, irrational, or inappropriate.

If you deny or suppress your feelings, for whatever reason, you will never quite get over them. I advocate that you first let yourself feel petty, selfish, demanding, irrational, and inappropriate, and then learn to express your feelings *without using force*. If you allow yourself to feel these "childlike" feelings, and yet don't act like a spoiled brat, you gain the capacity to heal from the feelings and become more powerful, and also engender honesty and forgiveness in others.

People will tend to respond to you on the level from which you speak. Recently, a man got on an elevator with me and said, "Hot enough for you?" Automatically, I uttered a similar cliché: "It's not the heat, it's the humidity." Conversely, when a person's communication is authentic, our response tends to be authentic as well. You will find that it's easier to forgive individuals who "come clean" with us as opposed to people who defend their actions with some self-serving rationale.

In order to tell someone what you sincerely want (a big part of your truth), you'll need to allow your petty, selfish, irrational, demanding side to come through harmlessly in your speaking. Without allowing yourself to feel and express these childlike things, your listener will feel forced to do what you want because you were so reasonable. How might you express your desires in such a way that the listener doesn't feel forced to comply with them? It takes a little practice to do this.

One of my clients recently told her husband that he needed to attend their kids' soccer games. "The kids really need you to be at their soccer game. All the other dads will be there," she said. After realizing that she was using guilt to manipulate him, she decided to tell the truth instead and said, "Even if the kids don't care either way, I care. I also want you to take them there so I can get a break this Saturday."

Even though the truth sounded a bit selfish, it was also honest, less guilt inducing, and less manipulative. The husband was more open to the truth because it did not put him on the defensive. In fact, his wife's honesty evoked a gracious response. "That's fine; I'll take them," he said.

Childlike, Not Childish

You'll note a paradox here in that I seem to be advocating childish behavior to help you become a more powerful adult. I'm not. It is childish to yell, act out, slam doors, attack people, use insults and sarcasm, withhold love, or embarrass others in order to get them to feel badly and change their behavior. Unfortunately, adults often operate that way. The ones who do are being spoiled brats. Such actions are blatant uses of force, and I'm not advocating or condoning such behavior.

However, if you allow yourself to feel whatever it is that you feel, even if it seems immature or childlike, you will be better off. The goal is to express those childlike feelings responsibly rather than acting out or using force. By expressing your feelings truthfully within a context of healing, you will be released from the harmful effects of such suppressed feelings. You will become powerful beyond measure. You will be restored to your childhood innocence.

CHAPTER **7**

Why Punishment Doesn't Work in Relationships

What you will learn from this chapter:

How to avoid punishing others or getting punished

How Do We Teach Each Other?

For many years, the prevailing wisdom said that the fastest way to get a person to learn something was to reward the individual for doing something right and to punish him or her for doing something wrong. It just seemed like common sense.

In the 1930s, however, a psychologist named B.F. Skinner created a special box (the Skinner box) to test this theory using laboratory rats and pigeons as subjects. The box had a lever inside of it which, when pressed by the animal, would dispense a food pellet (reward for desired behavior). It also had wire bars on the floor which could be electrified to administer a small shock (punishment for undesired behavior). What he found was rather surprising. The fastest learning did not happen when punishment and reward were used as feedback following behavior. *The fastest learning happened when undesirable behavior was ignored and the desired behavior (or some approximation thereof) was followed by a food pellet.*

The results were surprising, considering the widespread use of punishment in schools where learning was the objective. Nevertheless, Skinner was able to teach the animals an amazing array of tasks without the use of punishment. By linking the behaviors together, he was able to get a rat to pull a chain, then climb a ladder, ring a bell, and run on a treadmill before approaching the lever, depressing it and receiving a food pellet. Any undesirable behaviors were ignored. Only those that approximated the behaviors Skinner wanted were reinforced with food.

Ignore the bad stuff

There are obvious implications for human behavior in Skinner's work. One is simply to avoid commenting on or focusing on your partner's behaviors that annoy or upset you. Instead, appreciate your partner's qualities and focus on everything about him or her that you like. If Skinner's theory is correct, the undesirable behavior will diminish, and the behaviors you like will increase with the use of positive reinforcement. The option is certainly worth a try.

What about the efficacy of punishment?

From testing the Skinner box, other researchers have found that following an animal's undesirable behavior with some noxious stimulus like an electric shock (punishment) impeded the learning process instead of aiding it. After being shocked several times for wrong behaviors, the animals refused to participate in the experiments at all. Seemingly, they weren't willing to risk any behavior because of the chance they would get shocked for the wrong one.

Determined to entice the lab rats to make the right move, the researchers tried *negative reinforcement*. They placed their subjects on an electrified grid that continuously shocked the rat until the correct response was made. After which, the shock would immediately cease. (This reminds me of an old poster that said, "The beatings will continue until morale improves!") Even with the electrified grid, the rats still wouldn't budge.

To force the correct behavior, the experimenters then turned the juice up even higher until they were almost roasting the animals. The rats sat still, taking the shock and eventually defecating on themselves, yet never complying. I remember thinking as I was reading about these experiments that if the rats could talk, they would say, "We don't care what you do to us—we're *not playing!*"

I have found that punishment has the same effect on people. If someone appreciates your behavior on some occasions but sharply criticizes your mistakes at other times, your tendency will be to stop participating. I have worked with several couples when one partner complained that the mate never tried anything new in bed. When we talked about it further, the partner accused of being unimaginative would often refer back to a time when he or she did try something new and different only to be rebuked in a harsh tone: "What are you doing?" or "Don't! I don't like that!" When the breakdowns were never talked about and resolved, the adventurous partner had the same reaction as did the rats: "I'm not playing (or trying anything new) anymore." The rebuked partner then reverted to pedestrian, predictable sex so as to avoid painful criticism and ridicule.

Punishment Bypasses Life's Important Lessons

For optimal learning to take place, a person does something, gets to think about the consequences of the action, and, based on what has happened, chooses whether or not to engage in the behavior again.

Many years ago, as a school psychologist, I tested public school children using the Stanford-Binet Children's IQ test. My wooden briefcase had individual compartments for the dozens of tiny puzzle pieces, beads, rings, string, small wooden blocks, marbles, cardboard cards, toys, etc. for the tests. One day, I accidentally opened the briefcase upside down and everything inside went flying. It took me over an hour to get all the pieces back into the box in the correct sections. From that experience I learned to be highly cognizant of which side was up as I opened the briefcase. I never made that mistake again. While the experience wasn't pleasant, I had no one to blame except myself, and, thereafter, took responsibility for opening it correctly.

Punishment changes this dynamic. If punishment follows a mistake, especially a punishment that seems harsh or unfair, we might use it as an excuse to escape into a *revenge fantasy*.

For instance, I recently heard a preteen boy say, "I would never do that to my kid if I were a parent. I can't believe what an unfair bi***h she is for grounding me!" Rather than take responsibility for the consequences his actions brought about, the boy focused on his punisher. He brooded over how victimized and oppressed he was by his mom. None of these thoughts contributes to learning a more productive way to behave.

For couples, punishment tends to damage trust. Not only does it rarely lead to a satisfying result, but punishment is also a form of force. As we have shown, force begets force. So how can you prevent pushing back when you feel forced?

I often recommend sharing your fantasy of how you might like to punish the other person, but not doing it. Previously, when my wife has made light of something that upset me, I have said, "I feel like waiting until you are really upset about something, and then I'll just laugh it off. Then we'll see how *you* feel!" But I don't carry out that threat.

Talking about it is usually enough to relieve the need to act out. Wherever possible, replace punishment with truthful self-expression. Your relationship will be enhanced because of it. Remember, punishment, like most forms of force, moves you and your partner out onto the skinny branches of the tree. Things can be unstable out there. Self-expression (if done effectively) brings you back toward the trunk where things feel much more solid.

CHAPTER **8**

Context versus Content

What you will learn from this chapter:

How to distinguish between what people say and what they mean

Distinguishing Context from Content

Communication between people occurs on a number of levels. In every conversation and in every argument, you discuss something specific. This is the *content*. Content is easy to identify. It is the "nuts and bolts" of the conversation. For couples, it could be their children's behavior, the dishes, the amount of money one person is spending, what to wear to a social occasion, why the boss is annoying, etc.

The *context* of the conversation is another level of communication that has nothing to do with the particular content of the discussion. It consists of the tone of voice of the speaker; the proximity of each person to one another; the hand gestures, facial expressions, eye movements and body language of the speaker; where the conversation is taking place, etc. Generally, context concerns how the conversation feels emotionally. It has been said that context is the bowl in which the content is contained. It can greatly affect the outcome of your conversation. Therefore, it can greatly affect your relationship.

Consider, for example, how "I can hardly wait for your mother to get here" conveys an entirely different meaning when spoken sincerely as opposed to when it is spoken sarcastically. Here, the context, not the content, is what changes the communication.

Context Is King

When couples communicate, context is everything. It determines the outcome of the conversation in terms of intimacy and continued partnership regardless of the content. It doesn't matter what you discuss—if the context is not loving or at least neutral, the outcome will not enhance the relationship. Conversely, if the context is loving, the content will not matter that much. A context of love will enrich your relationship regardless of the decision you reach from the discussion.

I felt the full power of context during a particularly uncomfortable interaction with my wife. Driving in the direction of a few restaurants one night, she and

I were discussing where to dine. I was becoming annoyed with Lauren because I wanted her to choose but didn't think that she was giving me a clear decision. I said, in an annoyed tone of voice (context), "Look, if you want Chinese, just say *Chinese*. If you want Italian, say *Italian*!"

My wife responded, "Jimmy, I don't feel like we are on the same team." This wasn't the answer I was looking for.

Her reply was on the contextual level (same team), but I wanted content in her response (which restaurant). I said, forcing the issue back to content, "Does that mean Chinese?"

She responded, "I don't feel like it matters what we decide if we aren't on the same team. I don't think we'll enjoy ourselves."

Not to be outdone, I answered, "Do you want to go back home?"

She said, "No, I don't think it would matter. We'd still not be on the same team. I just want to be on the same team with you. Once we are on the same team, I feel like we'll enjoy ourselves wherever we go even if the food isn't fantastic."

I realized at that moment how powerful context is and how powerful a person becomes by keeping an eye on the context of the conversation and refusing to be drawn into content when the context is unfriendly.

By drawing your attention to the context rather than focusing on content, you will be in a better position to attend to your relationship. Rather than fixating on a particular item being argued about, you'll more likely end up on the "same team" if one of you stays on this level of context until the relationship is on better footing.

CHAPTER **9**

Four Channels of Truth

What you will learn from this chapter:

How to express your irrefutable truth

From studying my children and observing thousands of hours of adult conversation, I've discovered that the whole truth can be expressed in four ways.

These are:

1. What you like

2. What you want

3. How you feel

4. What you don't like

Each of these categories or channels complies with our definition of the truth in that, once a truth has been expressed, the listener will not be able to debate or argue with what has just been said. I used to believe that these four channels were weighted equally in terms of their ability to restore us to our natural state of happiness. I no longer believe that.

For instance, if you persist in focusing on and expressing what you don't like in terms of complaints, criticisms or rants, you will become more and more aware of these things and will begin to feel worse and worse over time. Conversely, if you consistently focus on what you like and express appreciation for those things, your mood and perspective will brighten considerably as will your satisfaction with your relationship.

For this reason, I'm going to discuss these different channels of the truth in their order of importance for the purpose of feeling happy and satisfied. We'll put them in a different order when we get to the Four-Channel Clearing™ in Chapter 11.

What You Like

This channel is so important to good relationships that if you devoted your whole life to expressing what you like and what you appreciate, you might not ever have to deal with the other aspects of your truth.

Human beings, by virtue of their ability to make distinctions, can form preferences. They can determine what they like and what they don't like. You'll find that telling people what you like is a great way to share yourself without offending anyone. You aren't telling them what they should like and you are not telling them that what you like is good or better than what they like. I recommend commenting on anything that pleases you by saying, "I like that." For instance, "I like your hair" or "I like that style of front porch" or "I like apple cider" changes your mood in a positive direction and has a connective effect on any relationship.

Here is an interesting by-product of this channel: The more you express what you like, the happier you will become. That last statement, although it is my assertion, is quite profound if you think about it. It means that you have control over how happy you feel simply by where you place your focus. Conversely, if you continue to focus on what you don't like, you will notice that you have become more and more unhappy. The good news is that we all have a choice.

There is one caveat to mention about stating what you like. If you repeatedly point out things you like that are the opposite of what your partner has to offer, your communication will probably not be well received. If your partner has a large belly and you keep saying, "I really like washboard abs and tiny waists," this will be perceived as hurtful. If your partner has a high school education and you keep saying, "I like college educated people. I find them so fascinating," this won't go over well, either. Use common sense here.

I Like What You Did or Said

Talking about what we like takes a different form when referring to something that another person said or did. The sentence with the most impact is one that is transitive in nature i.e., it travels directly from one person to another.

When someone does or says something that we like, the most powerful way to express that is by saying, "I appreciate you for (some fact)." For example, "I appreciate you for taking out the trash" or "I appreciate you for saying that you liked the dessert I made better than the kind you can get at the store."

Remember that appreciations are personal and have the greatest impact when stated in the form, "I appreciate you for [x]." When the speaker says, "I appreciate *you* for your sense of humor," he produces a different experience for the listener and for himself than when he says, "I appreciate *your* sense of humor or I appreciate *the fact that* you have a sense of humor."

The more you practice saying appreciations, the more you'll notice how much you appreciate people and the better you will feel. As long as the appreciations are not used to avoid saying some other withheld truth, you'll find that they tend to engender love and forgiveness in a relationship.

Noticing what you appreciate and expressing appreciations to the people around you tends to keep you in a state of gratitude. The interesting thing about gratitude is that it counteracts fear. You'll find that it is hard to be fearful and grateful at the same time.

How to Just Be Happy

One way to transform your relationship and your life completely is to just be happy. If you work on where you put your focus, notice and comment on what you like and appreciate people for everything they say or do that you like, your life will change rather dramatically.

If you can develop what is commonly known as an *attitude of gratitude*, this will color all of your perceptions and interpretations. Your partner will look more physically appealing, their issues will be viewed more compassionately and you'll find that you have less and less reason to complain about him or her.

If you spend time doing what brings you joy and thinking about things that make you smile, you'll spend most of your time feeling happy. It sounds simplistic but it really works. Even if you are with a person who does or says things you don't like, try focusing and talking about the aspects of them that you do like and admire and those characteristics will become predominant in your thinking.

How You Feel

This is an extremely important part of telling the truth, and for some people, it's the area that is the most unclear. Many people confuse *how they feel* with *what they think*. "I feel okay" or "I feel that you are wrong" are statements that don't quite get at the unchallengeable truth of our experience.

So how do we tell the truth about our feelings?

Just say as many adjectives that come to mind to describe how you feel. Don't say "I feel sad because..." Say, "I feel sad." Once you say "...because," you will launch into the reasons which justify or legitimize your feelings and you will no longer be telling the irrefutable truth. Someone somewhere could argue with your reasons. Keep it simple. *I feel...* [adjective or adjective phrase]. An example of an adjective phrase would be, "I feel like I can't win for trying."

On the most basic level, we can all report our feelings as bodily sensations. These sensations, when stated simply and unambiguously, can be understood by anyone. Pain, burning, temperature, stiffness, sweating, chills, shortness of breath, pressure in the chest, queasiness, etc., can be used to communicate our feelings to others. When people say, "I feel nauseated," we know what they are talking about.

The Adjective List

In Table 1, you'll find a list of adjectives and adjective phrases grouped by category. I've expanded this list over the years to include as many types of feelings as I could identify. I recommend you use it as follows: First, think of an issue you have with another person. Ask yourself, *With regard to that issue how do I feel*? Use the list to find the category or categories of emotions that your feelings fall into e.g., VICTIMIZED or ANGRY, then peruse the adjectives in that list until one of them sort of jumps out at you. Once you have identified the correct feeling, just say, *I feel patronized* or *I feel misled*. This is your irrefutable truth. Say, *I feel... [fill in adjective]* as many times as necessary to get all of the feelings out of your system. Remember that it is quite possible to feel patronized or misled whether or not the other person is trying to patronize or mislead you.

In talking to a partner, a person might say, "I feel [fill in adjective]..." as many as ten times. For example, *I feel sad, I feel disappointed, I feel let down, I feel tired, I feel discouraged, I feel angry, I feel vindictive, I feel duped.* It's important to keep saying, "I feel" before every few adjectives rather than just listing them in a long string.

I'm Afraid that...

Underlying the majority of negative feelings is the most basic of all: fear. Beneath our anger, hurt, shame, depression, or discomfort is often something about which we are afraid. It may be an unreasonable fear, but is still true for us. When we can identify a fear, the best way to express it is: *I'm afraid that...* Use the first channel, **How I Feel**, to empty your mind of whatever it is that you might be afraid of.

For example, say, "I'm afraid that you will keep spending and spending until we have to declare bankruptcy" or "I'm afraid you will stop loving me if I don't lose weight." Don't worry about how silly these fears might sound. Just say them and you'll be freed from having to act on those fears. Many controlling behaviors diminish when we can express our fears. The more we can identify, experience and express our feelings, the less inclined we are to act on them.

TABLE I: Adjectives Describing How You Feel

POSITIVE

UP — Good, happy, delighted, confident, joyous, conscientious, cheerful, compassionate, joyous, blessed, loved, excited, optimistic, encouraged, heartened, hopeful, interested, interesting, positive, silly, carefree, giddy, playful, open, honored, admired, esteemed, prosperous, adored, cherished, paid-attention-to, proud, appealing, noticed, loving, perfect, awe-struck, impressed, articulate, clear, high, blissful, lovable, cheerful, wonderful, smart, magnificent, fantastic, clear, ahead, safe, hopeful, pleased, delighted

GRATITUDE — Grateful, gratified, thankful, appreciated, blessed, hopeful, like a spoiled grandchild, special, doted on, appreciative, lucky, adoring, indebted, admiring, thanked, loved, graced, anointed, valued

PEACE — *Generous, kind, pure, sincere, calm, fortunate, relieved, natural, trusted, loved, satisfied, content, blessed, pleased, forgiven, pardoned, forgiving, accepted, accepting, connected, taken-care-of, healed, healthy, trustful, trustworthy, mellow, secure, appreciated, appreciative, rewarded, free, present, attentive, respected, redeemed, peaceful, centered, validated, acknowledged, understood, thanked, released, patient, full, relieved, open*

COMFORTABLE — *Centered, rested, relaxed, cozy, refreshed, yummy, at ease, free, warm, toasty*

POWERFUL — *On track, in control, disciplined, competent, capable, able, structured, protected, intentional, victorious, organized, on schedule, secure, bold, exonerated, brave, certain, determined, confident, important, self-reliant, engaged, intrepid, strong, valiant, vibrant, on top of things, lucid, passionate, guilt proof, invincible*

EXCITED — *Exuberant, boisterous, adventurous, enthusiastic, exhilarated, zestful, zany, zealous, thrilled, passionate, energized, invigorated, engaged, playful, sexual, horny, eager, ecstatic, jazzed, fired up, ready*

INTERESTED — *Intrigued, curious, amused, open, fascinated, awestruck, blown away, enthralled, captivated, dazzled, bemused*

NEUTRAL — *Full, warm, cold, sleepy, tired, restless, bored, fuzzy-headed, cautious, eager, sensitive, stimulated, alert, responsible, hungry, thirsty, spent, quizzical, open*

NEGATIVE

VICTIMIZED — *Jerked-around, forced, manipulated, pressured, blamed, wrongly accused, victimized, violated, slimed, dominated, shut-out, attacked, slighted, screwed-over, set-up, criticized, judged, disrespected, put-down, put-upon, picked-on, ridiculed, ill-advised, mistreated, lied-to, misled, withheld-from, deceived, overworked, cornered, ambushed, laughed at, sabotaged, punished, unfairly treated, patronized, dumped, rejected, left-out, ganged-up-on, double-teamed, pitied, shunned, trapped, done-unto, used, tricked, not-considered, oppressed, embarrassed, "rode hard and put away wet", burned*

DOWN — *Sorry, blue, sad, hurt, depressed, hopeless, pessimistic, negative, weak, unlovable, worthless, useless, stupid, sorry-for-myself, miserable, circling-the-rim, disappointed, suicidal, depleted, enervated, like-I-want-to-go-to-sleep-and-never-wake-up, like-I-am-corkscrewing-myself-into-the-ground, pathetic, like a loser*

STUCK OR POWERLESS — *Trapped, between-a-rock-and-a-hard-place, like-I'm-a-day-late-and-a-dollar-short, hopeless, helpless, can't-get-there-from-here, powerless, doomed, resigned, frustrated, exasperated, thwarted, defeated, confused, coping, unsure, unclear, out of control, paralyzed, checkmated, stalemated, like-I'm-treading-water, feckless, confused, floundering, befuddled, confounded, over-burdened*

UNCOMFORTABLE — *Restless, tense, frustrated, anxious, tightness in my... (part of the body), concerned, hurt, sad, depressed, sick, weak, weakened, bored, nauseated, disgusting, agitated, uneasy, exhausted, tired, lost, overwhelmed, in-over-my-head, sneaky, unappreciated, unappreciative, driven, addicted, fidgety, impatient, reluctant, uncentered, unclear, confused, bewildered, unsure, jealous, envious, devious, sinister, spaced-out, absent-minded, bloated, constipated, troubled, shell-shocked, wary, spent, fragile, edgy, distressed, strained, embarrassed, undisciplined, off schedule, behind, pressured, overwhelmed*

FEAR — *Fearful, nervous, afraid, frantic, panicky, hysterical, horrified, worried, apprehensive, distressed, aghast, alarmed, uneasy, terrified, in-over-my-head, anxious, frightened, dismayed, dumbfounded, flabbergasted, unprotected, out-gunned, like-I'm-drowning*

SHAME *— Bad, wrong, guilty, evil, stupid, inarticulate, not-good-enough, insignificant, not trusted, unloved, not-special, ordinary, useless, unlovable, unappealing, embarrassed, humiliated, like-I-can-never-win-no-matter-what-I-do, unimportant, boring, like "What am I, chopped liver?", shamed, foolish, ashamed, isolated, alone, lonely, awful, inadequate, unwelcome, damaged, broken, insecure, careless, negligent, unreliable, at-fault, defective, poor, needy, wanting, unfortunate, dirty, unprepared, incompetent, responsible, unwanted, broken, like-I'm-a-failure*

ANGER *— Angry, furious, outraged, disgusted, vindictive, self-righteous, judgmental, hostile, closed, seething, indignant, catty, petty, selfish, punitive, angry, ornery, mean, nasty, hurtful, frosted, livid, jealous, like-a-ticking-bomb, pissed, annoyed, ticked-off*

DEFENSIVE *— Suspicious, petty, selfish, unconvinced, mischievous, disobedient, wary, leery, doubtful, closed, argumentative, contrary, catty, uneasy, negative, shut-down, distrustful, possessive, sneaky, ganged-up-on, devious, negative, paranoid, like-I'm-guilty-till-proven-innocent, tolerated, over-powered, dug-in, protective*

MISUNDERSTOOD — *Misheard, misquoted, like-my motives-were-being-impugned, invisible, unimportant, left-out, unacknowledged, wrongly accused, ignored, labeled, lumped-in-with-others, unappreciated, "dissed" or disrespected, disconnected, out-of-the-loop, in-the-dark, like nobody-understands-what-it feels-like-to-be-me-right-now, doubted, disbelieved, not trusted*

SURPRISED — *Shocked, aghast, flabbergasted, stymied, puzzled, amazed, astonished, incredulous, startled, ambushed, stunned, dazed, jolted, astounded, appalled, dumbfounded, horrified, jostled, shaken, jarred, non-plussed, perplexed, embarrassed*

Tuning In to How You Feel

In working with couples for many years and in examining the early dynamics of my own marriage, I was often amazed at our ability to repeat the same uncomfortable scenarios with each other. Often in the middle of a conversation where each one of us was holding firm to some position and the battle lines were being drawn, I would have the distinct feeling that I had been here before.

The content of the disagreement would be different but the dynamics were exactly the same. Each of us was using our favorite argument with evidence and witnesses ("I'm not the only one who feels this way!") to back up our position. Each time we'd end up in the same stuck place more convinced of the rightness of our point of view and the "wrongness" of our partner's.

Over time I saw a common thread to these conversations-*they never felt good*! Early on, it never dawned on me to check out how I was feeling during the wrestling match but as my consciousness has grown, I have developed a healthy distaste for continuing anything that doesn't feel good.

It was that discovery more than anything else that led me to find other ways of relating to my wife and other places to focus my attention than on her faults and shortcomings. I found that the more I focused on the things that I liked about her, the less often we would find ourselves on opposites sides of the ring. In fact, the more I paid attention to those aspects of her that I appreciated, the more of them I saw and the more compassion I developed for her when she was unhappy.

"I want to feel good" has become a mantra of sorts for me. I see now that I have a lot more control over how I feel than I ever knew was possible. I can choose where to place my attention and can choose to shut down familiar scenarios that don't lead to a good feeling. And

I do. I've found that a heightened awareness of what is really important leads to better choices in the brief time we have together on this planet.

What You Don't Like

Most of us have no trouble identifying what we don't like. We can easily determine what annoys, aggravates, irritates, or bothers us. That's the nature of a complaint. You've probably noticed that people have no trouble complaining. Letting people know what you don't like is useful information if they ever want to please or respect you. Once they find out what you don't like, they get a better idea of how you like to be treated and then learn what to avoid doing or saying in your presence.

For instance, my cousin doesn't like mushrooms. That's the irrefutable truth for him—not that there is anything wrong with mushrooms or him. He just doesn't like them. Who cares? Anyone planning to make a meal for him to enjoy would care. I guarantee you that if there are mushrooms in the dish, he won't touch it! (Fred always asks about the possible presence of mushrooms before tasting a new dish).

Likewise, if your spouse doesn't like surprises, you can avoid upset and wasted effort by not planning a surprise birthday party for him or her even if it's a special birthday. On this level, what a person doesn't like is useful information to help you understand the individual and enables you to respect his or her boundaries.

When things happen that we don't like, our response is often anger or annoyance. Anger is a powerful and often dangerous emotion when not handled appropriately. Unchecked, it can lead to hurtful words, hurtful actions, and sometimes violence. Most relationships end with unresolved anger even if, on the surface, it seems as though two people have just grown apart. Suppressing anger doesn't work particularly well, and expressing it inappropriately can often make things worse. Anger has to be handled with considerable consciousness, and this takes practice. I request that you read all the way through the next section before practicing any of this communication process or deciding whether to accept or reject any ideas.

Expressing Resentment

Resentment has often been wryly defined as *a poison pill that we take with the hope that the other person will die.* When we are young and our boundaries are violated, when we feel disrespected, unimportant, unfairly treated or hurt, we don't like it. Underneath the initial feelings of anger and hurt we may wonder, *Did I do something wrong to get myself treated this way*? As

Four Channels of Truth

we grow older, we learn quickly to project these guilty feelings onto others. (We'll talk about why this happens later.) We hold them responsible for our feelings and our situation, and feel justified in attacking them in some way. We try to push the blame onto others in the hopes that our own feelings of guilt will be dissipated. As the poison pill example illustrates, resentments hurt us much more than the person with whom we are angry.

For this reason, The Four-Channel Clearing™ (discussed in Chapter 11) focuses on helping us release our anger and resentment so that we can access the love and connection again. Suppressing our feelings or rationalizing them away ultimately kills our passion and spontaneity. Attacking someone when we are angry will never lead to healing; if anything, it makes it harder to get back on the same team.

How can we, then, release these intense feelings and not make things worse?

Out of the Mouths of Babes

If you let younger children express themselves when they are angry, they usually tell you what happened (the facts), and then they tell you how they feel about what happened. For example, a boy might say to his brother, "Billy, you knocked my fort down...*and I didn't like that!*" The child certainly does not hold back on the last part! He lets Billy know how angry he is.

Somehow, when little children tell the truth, the intensity of their feelings do not feel like an attack to the listener. Witnessing such a release, you might liken the episode to fireworks being fired straight up in the air. It may be loud and intense, but as long as the explosion isn't aimed at you, it's not dangerous.

In contrast, if someone directs his or her anger at us in the form of an attack, the relationship we have with the person will suffer, and further healing communication will be unlikely.

I adopted the method I saw my children use when they were little as the best format for **What I Don't Like**. This method works well for most of us by allowing us to express our anger truthfully in a way that is healing and not hurtful to the listener.

A Safe Way to Express Resentments

"You did or said [some fact] and I didn't like that!"

For example: "You left the dirty frying pan on the counter, and I didn't like that. I ended up scraping it and cleaning it just before my parents got here, and I didn't like that either." Once you get on a roll, you can go over anything you bring to mind that happened and follow it up with and *I didn't like that, either!*

Check with your partner to learn if he or she is okay if you put some emotion behind the latter part of the sentence. If your partner feels safe, then allow yourself to feel angry as you are saying it. The more you can experience while telling the truth, the easier it will be to let the anger go.

Additionally, you may express anger in the first person (by using I) as long as the statement is factual. "I don't like the way you are looking at me right now" or "I don't like talking about my feelings unless they are positive."

Don't paraphrase with a sentence like "I didn't like being set up to look bad." Instead, talk about what exactly happened, "I didn't like you telling your Mom she could come over before I got home. She got here while the house was still a mess. I felt embarrassed to have her see it when it wasn't straightened up and I felt set up by you." (It's okay to add a few more feelings if you notice any while expressing your resentments).

Instead of saying, "I didn't like that you said I looked tired and worn out," say, "I didn't like that you said (imitating the way you heard it), 'You look tired and worn out.'" It's always better to quote someone directly while imitating their tone of voice than to describe their tone and what they said in the passive voice.

What if your partner does not feel safe listening to your angry feelings?

Sometimes, just listening to someone else being angry, even if the words are not aimed at you, can feel awful. If you and your partner have a history of scary, inappropriate or abusive expressions of anger, then the best thing to do is to let the angry party go somewhere private. There, he or she will tell the truth to the four walls while letting as much steam off as possible.

Since I was the hothead in my family, I would often go out to my car, close all the windows, and let my resentments be unleashed until they held no more charge. Then I'd come back and do the Four-Channel Clearing™ with Lauren. With much of the venom removed from my system, we'd move through the process much more easily.

What Lies Beneath the Anger?

Anger is neither a fundamental nor basic emotion, but it is often a cover for something deeper. After you express your resentments, notice how you feel. There will most likely be something present for you, such as sadness, hurt, embarrassment, guilt, shame, fear, etc. It is valuable to express these feelings, when you feel them, without explanation or justification. As we have discussed previously, just say, "I feel [fill in the adjective]." At this point, you may become aware of something for which you appreciate your partner—perhaps right in the middle of your diatribe!—and suddenly have trouble continuing with your resentments. That's not unusual. Express the appreciation. Then, if needed, return to what the other did or said that you didn't like.

While the other three channels—how you feel, what you want, and what you like—can sometimes be expressed with or without the rest of the channels, resentment and anger (what you don't like) should be used only as part of The Four-Channel Clearing™, which includes a preamble (Chapter 10). Anger needs a preamble plus the other aspects of the truth to be transformed into forgiveness.

What You Want

The most potent way to express what you want is to do so directly. For example, "I want you to take me with you" or "I want you to surprise me with flowers when it's not even my birthday."

The power of this message depends on whether you can convey what you want in a way that the other person does not feel forced to give it to you (a demand that doesn't feel like one). This can be tricky since most demands are perceived as some sort of implied force. That's why it's important to get others to understand that *they don't have to do what you say—you just want them to.* If your partner responds with, "And what if I don't?" you can say that there will be no adverse consequences; the worst thing that will happen is that you will continue to tell the truth until you feel better and get over what is bothering you.

This particular channel offers the most effective way of changing the dance between people. Like the other channels, it allows your partner to know what is true for you (what you really want) and, more importantly, it sets the stage for him or her to comply if he or she chooses.

This Can't Possibly Work

We have come to the most challenging part of teaching the principles of *Powerful Partnerships*® for me—convincing people to start asking for what they want without using force or manipulation to get it. Most people can't imagine this would ever work. "Why would someone do what I want just because it would make me happy?" People would rather bolster their wants with reasons, legitimacy, logic, fairness, needs, justifications, urgency, guilt, shame, morals, and a host of additional excuses—all of which are perceived as force by the other person. This is why we often don't get what we want, even from people who profess to love us: they can't get past the force.

I invite you to use this channel and just see what happens. Remember, force gets an immediate response. If you'd like to test this assertion, try making an obscene gesture to someone in traffic and watch how quickly force begets force.

Unlike force, however, the effects of using power often don't show up immediately. Powerful communication takes a little while to take root in another person and start growing. It requires a little patience. Yet, the payoffs are huge.

The Value of Absurdity

The best way to keep people from feeling forced when you tell them what you want is to be unreasonable or ridiculous. That way, they will be less likely to feel guilty if they don't do what you want.

"Why do you have to watch TV all day?" The question makes a person feel bad and wrong for being a couch potato. And the truth might be surprising: "I want you to turn off the TV and pay attention to me. I want you to find me so fascinating that TV holds no interest for you. I also want you to follow me around anticipating and meeting my every need and enjoy doing it."

Someone listening to that, thinking you have obviously lost your mind, will not feel defensive. If you say this often enough, your partner may even start to make efforts in your direction. Remember: *Telling the truth of your experience—not manipulating the other person into doing what you want—is what heals you.*

Off the Ridiculometer

Once I understood that the other person didn't have to do what I wanted, I was thrilled to find out that I was no longer constrained by reasonableness. In fact, I was finally free to ask for what I *really* wanted and didn't have to edit my comments to make sure they made sense.

For instance, with a straight face, I once said this to Lauren, "Honey, I would like to be able to interrupt you at any time, whether you are on the phone, in the bathroom, talking to someone in the yard, concentrating on some project, whatever. I'd just like you to stop what you're doing immediately and pay attention to me. So, for instance, while talking on the phone to the White House you would say, 'Excuse me, Mr. President. Yes, Jim?' and give me your undivided attention without me ever having to wait."

I believe her response was, "Oh, really?"

"Yes, that's right," I said. "Also, when I am on the phone, in the bathroom, playing the piano, or doing something else, I'd like you never to interrupt me. Just wait patiently until I have finished before talking to me."

She said, "Dream on! That's a ridiculous double standard and is not going to happen in this lifetime."

I said, "I didn't say you *had* to. It would just make me very happy if you did."

She said something like, "It would make me very happy if I had my own TV talk show but that's not going to happen either."

I said, "That's okay. If you wake up some morning and want to make my day this would do it. I want to be allowed to interrupt you anytime but you never interrupt me."

After that, she just gave me a look like what I was asking for was off the "ridiculometer." It was. So what? If she thought it was stupid, she didn't have to do it.

Months later, after asking for this repeatedly, I noticed that she tended to let me interrupt her without complaining and often waited before interrupting me. This is still going on. I don't think she even realized that the shift had taken place.

Wanting What Is Fair and Reasonable Equals Force

Any time you ask for something you want and it is accompanied by the expressed or unexpressed belief on your part of *that's not so much to ask*, there is force in the message. You believe your request is modest or reasonable, and, therefore, should be granted. This won't work. Feeling the force, your partner will not want to do what you want.

If you begin your request by saying something like, "Now, you know that I rarely ask you for anything…" you are implying that this one time when you are asking for something, the least the other could do is fulfill your wishes. She/he owes you that. This won't work either. *Quid pro quo* feels like force. You can't fake the "and you don't have to" part. Non-compliance has to be okay with you. The other must feel like he or she has the freedom to be gracious. If you give that freedom, I can't guarantee that your partner will comply, but at least he or she will get to choose freely. Usually, out of being in relationship with you, the other will want to do what you want (unless the individual is strongly opposed to it). By the way, no matter how many times you sweetly and without force ask people to cut off an arm, they are unlikely to comply. This isn't just because what you want is unreasonable or because they don't love you. The reason is that *you are asking them to do something they don't want to do.*

Do You Really Mean It?

"Do you really mean it?" This is a good question to ask yourself before you ask for what you want: *Is it really okay if they don't do what I want? Are there no consequences for them if they don't comply with my demand?* If you examine what you want from another person, you'll find that it isn't just compliance you're seeking. You want people to *want to do* what you want—willingly, lovingly, and cheerfully! Anything else may reap some sort of negative effect down the line. Either you will feel like you now owe the other person something *(quid pro quo)*, or you will expect some form of force returning to you from the individual at some time.

Requests versus Wants

Remember that asking for what you want is not a request. A request elicits one of three responses from a person right away: (1) Yes; (2) No; or (3) Some sort of counter proposal. For example, "Will you drive me to soccer practice tomorrow?" might elicit "Okay" or "No" or "How about if you get a ride there, and I'll pick you up after practice and bring you home?" Wants are different.

Planting a Seed and Waiting for It to Grow

Asking for what you want powerfully doesn't require an immediate answer, so don't ask for one if you can avoid it. You just put out what you want; your partner will either do it or they won't. You have to be okay either way or they will feel the force.

"Look, you don't have to do this, but I'm going to be driving out to check on that rental property this afternoon. If you feel like it, I'd love it if you'd come with me." Then you wait and see what happens. The answer might be *No* at first. If so, you can say, "I understand. You don't have to. If you change your mind, let me know." It takes a while for others to get that you aren't forcing them.

The process is much like planting a seed and waiting to see if it sprouts. Give it some time. If you dig the seed up every day to see if it has germinated yet, it won't ever germinate. Be patient and keep asking for what you want with the same reassurances that they don't have to do it. Often when others experience the freedom of being asked to do something with no manipulation or force involved, they may eventually comply. Or they may not. Either way, you will feel better having told the truth and, in the process, released your attachment to a particular outcome.

Keep Asking As If You Never Asked Previously

Don't be surprised if you end up asking for what you want again and again. If you still want it and haven't gotten what you asked for, ask again. Each time you ask, be careful to leave the force out of it. For example, steer clear of saying (with annoyance in your voice), "For the 999th time, I want you to close the bathroom door when you have the fan on!" This will be felt as force: "You should have done what I wanted by now since I've asked so many times." This will most likely get your partner to resist what you want because he or she can feel the force behind your words. Instead, ask for what you want as if you never asked for it before.

"By the way, I'd like you to close the bathroom door when the fan is on (spoken as if you never mentioned this before)."

"Yes, I know. You've told me that."

"Well, it's something that is still important to me. If you wake up some morning and want to make me happy, that would do it. And you don't have to."

Over time, the process will have an effect on your partner. Unless you are asking for something that the individual absolutely does not want to do, he or she will probably do it while thinking it was his or her idea.

Keep practicing. Don't say, "I asked you to do this and you still haven't done it!" They might come back with, "I thought you said I didn't have to!" Plant the seed and don't dig it up right away to see if it has sprouted. Ask for much more than you have a right to expect if it's what you want. You have nothing to lose (other than people thinking you are absurd) and everything to gain.

CHAPTER **10**

Setting the Stage for The Four-Channel Clearing

What you will learn from this chapter:

How to create the ideal context for healing

In *Powerful Partnerships*® I have devised a technique for full self-expression in all four previously mentioned pathways of truth. It's called The Four-Channel Clearing™.

The following chapter (Chapter 11) will go into the mechanics of the Four-Channel Clearing™ in detail. However, before beginning this process, the stage must be set so that the person listening to the Four-Channel Clearing™ is open to what is being said. For this reason, the exercise always begins with a preamble.

The Preamble

The preamble is vital to the success of The Four-Channel Clearing™. It is used to establish a context for healing. Your goal in the preamble is to let your partner know why it is in his or her best interest to hear you out. If you approach someone and say to them, "Listen, I have a bone to pick with you. When would you have time to talk?" don't be surprised if the person is not particularly open to speaking with you any time soon. As far as the other is concerned, it is not in his or her best interest to hear you out. The fear is that you will use this occasion to express anger or disappointment, scold, or make the person wrong in some way. You have created an unsafe context, and the individual will want no part of what you are attempting to do.

What you say in the preamble is designed to put another at ease so he or she can listen without being on the defensive to your truth. Imagine how you would feel if, in the preamble, your partner said the following: "I notice that I'm not feeling very close to you. I want to say what is true for me so that I can get over what's bothering me and feel close to you again."

Wouldn't you be more willing to continue listening?

The preamble is used to assure the other person that you are taking full responsibility for healing yourself and that you will not use this session as a chance to shame, blame, or attack because of your upset feeling, for example: "I know this might sound irrational but it's still true for me. I just want to say this so it can feel better about you," or "I know that this is my stuff, so you don't have to dignify what I'm going to say with a defense."

The preamble is also the place for you to reveal how you feel about what you are about to say, for example, "I'm afraid you are going to hate me [reject me, think less of me, etc.] for having these feelings and wanting what I want."

What you are assuring your partner is that in the Four-Channel Clearing™ you are going to get over what is bothering you by (1) owning what is true for you, and (2) expressing your truth without making the individual bad or wrong and without using force.

All the other person is required to do is watch and listen. In fact, invite your partner to cut you off if you say anything which he or she could dispute or disagree. If you do this correctly and just tell the irrefutable truth, the individual won't feel inclined to interrupt you or walk away in the middle of your monologue. If your partner interrupts, it will be good feedback for you; it will help you restate your truth in a way that cannot be debated. Furthermore, ask your partner to cut you off if he or she feels force of any kind. In response to being interrupted by your partner, promise to rephrase your words so that the other party does not feel compelled or coerced into admitting or doing anything.

Continue the preamble until the other person gives you the "green light" to proceed with the Four-Channel Clearing^{tm}. If the other party says, "Okay, I'm fine with whatever you need to tell me; I'm not going to hate you or get up in the middle of your talk," that is your green light. If they sound impatient and make corresponding hand gestures (conveying, "Okay, okay, okay. Get on with it, already!"), that's even better. You know you have done the preamble well.

Important: continue your preamble until the other person urges you to move on.

CHAPTER **11**

The Four-Channel Clearing In Action

What you will learn from this chapter:

How to transform upset feelings into forgiveness

The Four-Channel Clearing™ is something that partners can do when they feel upset with each other or stuck in some way. It allows people to state their truth by expressing whatever they feel, using each of the four channels in a certain order: how they feel, what they don't like, what they want, and what they like. By doing the Four-Channel Clearing™, they can responsibly express everything that is true for them with regard to a particular issue without resorting to force and thereby bring about their own healing in the presence of another person. After clearing out whatever was in those channels, their experience is transformed and they are no longer upset. More often than not, they are restored to the love they have for the other person and for themselves.

The best time to initiate a Four-Channel Clearing™ is when you notice that you don't feel close to your partner anymore. This could be the result of an argument that was never resolved, something they said or did that you didn't like or for reasons you can't explain.

If you aren't upset with--or feeling distant from--your partner, then it's fine to express what you like and how you feel and what you want (without using force, of course).

THE PREAMBLE FReeWAy™

To make it easier to remember how to proceed with The Four-Channel Clearing™, I have devised an acronym called The Preamble **FR**ee**WA**y.

Each capital letter in **FR**ee**WA**y stands for a channel:

Feelings (how you feel)

Resentments (what you don't like)

Wants (what you want)

Appreciations (what you like).

It's not just the **FR**ee**WA**y; it's the **Preamble FR**ee**WA**y to remind you that before beginning to tell the truth, you need to begin with a preamble to set the stage for healing to take place.

The Four-Channel Clearing In Action

Following a Script

Here is a simple script to follow as you do the Four-Channel Clearing™. I recommend going over the details of the clearing ahead of time, writing down specific factual statements and keeping this script on your lap during the exercise to refer to. Over time, with practice, you won't need to refer to your notes when doing the clearing.

Preamble:

> As mentioned in the previous chapter, the preamble is critical to the success of the exercise. Establish the context for healing. Give your partner a good reason for hearing you out. One of the best ones is, "I don't feel close to you and I'd like to express myself so I can get over what is bothering me and feel good about you again." Include any fears you might have about embarking on the conversation you are about to have. "I'm afraid you'll think what I'm upset about is stupid."
>
> Promise to shoot your fireworks straight up and refrain from attack.
>
> Tell them they can interrupt if they feel force or hear anything that isn't true.

Continue the preamble until you get the green light from your partner that it is now alright to head down the **FReeWA**y.

How You Feel (**F**eelings)

Use the adjective list from Table 1 (holding it on your lap is fine) or go over it ahead of time to gather feelings.

"I feel... (adjective)." Don't just recite a list of adjectives. Say, "I feel sad, I feel hurt, I feel depressed," etc.

What You Didn't Like (**R**esentments)

"You did [some fact] and I didn't like that."

"You said [some sentence] and I didn't like that."

"[Something factual happened] and I didn't like that, either."

"I didn't like sitting in his office for almost an hour not knowing where you were."

Quote them directly rather than paraphrasing their words.

What You Want (**W**ants)

"You don't have to do this, but this is what I want."

Try to ask for more than is reasonable, more than a normal person would have the right to expect. The more unreasonable, ridiculous, outrageous and absurd your wants are the better. "I want you to say, 'Alice, you were right and I was wrong' so often that it sounds like a mantra (music to my ears) and then I want you to spend the rest of your life making it up to me."

Never say, "All I want is..." If it is reasonable to expect that they would do what you want, the other person will feel the force of your argument and won't comply.

What You Like (Appreciations**)**

"I appreciate you for [some specific fact]."

"I appreciate you for how safe I felt with you driving."

"I appreciate you for picking me up at my Mom's."

"I appreciate you for how you look right now."

"I appreciate you for saying, 'I'll finish cleaning up in the garage.'"

When you are done, see if you wouldn't mind hugging the other person. See if you can say, "I totally 100% forgive you for how uncomfortable I felt sitting in that guy's office for an hour not knowing where you were." If you can, then the Four-Channel Clearing™ worked and you are complete. If not, you need to go back and see what else there is to say or reiterate in one of the four channels. Eventually, you will have cleared everything out and you will be able to forgive your partner.

How to Listen to the Truth

One of the benefits of having a committed partner is that you can both agree to things and then hold each other to those promises. I always ask couples to agree to recognize force and to stop using it on each other.

That means that the person on the receiving end of The Four-Channel Clearing™ has a responsibility not to accept anything untrue that might be said. Often the speaker will throw in a little bit of their opinion along with their irrefutable truth. It is the responsibility of the listener not to accept it.

Hitting the Buzzer

I tell listeners to act as though they have a finger on a buzzer attached to the arm of their chair. As soon as they hear something that they want to take issue with, they "hit the buzzer" or make an obnoxious noise to interrupt the other person. Speakers have to rephrase what they said so their words come out as truth instead of something debatable.

I also advise listeners to hit their buzzer quickly if they start to feel the slightest bit of force in the conversation. Speakers have to reassure their listeners that they need not comply with anything asked for.

Buzzer Example

The following conversation contains some true and some less-than-true statements. Notice how the listener deflects the untrue statements and keeps things on track.

> Pat: "I was offended by your condescending attitude toward me when we were discussing that science fiction movie at the restaurant with our friends."

> Chris: "*Bzzzzzz*! I don't know what you are talking about." This is said in a calm, matter-of-fact tone of voice. "What did I do or say that you thought was condescending?"

By asking Pat to identify what was done or said, the facts are more likely to come out.

> Pat: "Well, I didn't like your tone of voice when you spoke to me in front of them."

> Chris: "Ok."

Notice how *condescending* wasn't a fact but *tone of voice* was. Chris did, indeed, have a particular tone of voice during that discussion at the restaurant, and Pat didn't like it. That's the truth of Pat's experience. It would have been even more effective if Pat, instead of paraphrasing, could have quoted Chris by imitating how the tone of voice sounded.

Later, Pat started using force. Chris again interrupted.

> Pat: "All I want is a little common courtesy and respect when we are in the company of our friends. I'm that way toward you. Is that too much to ask?"
>
> Chris: "*Bzzzzzz*! Feels like force to me!"

Pat's first sentence implied that any decent person *should* behave this way. *Should*, like *ought to* and *have to*, are moralistic judgments and feel like force to the listener. Can you recognize the force in Pat's seemingly innocent desire? That's enough to derail the healing effects of the truth right there.

Sometimes, in order for people to hear what you want and not feel forced, they have to know that you are being somewhat absurd and ridiculous in the way you state your desires. If you can communicate that you know that you are "over the top," they will feel less threatened and will be able to accept your absurd desire without defensiveness.

Non-Forceful Example

> Pat: "I want you to be so deferential and respectful when you speak to me, so in awe of my intelligence and wisdom, that everyone at the table is just blown away by it and one by one they come up to me later to comment on how loved and revered I am and how jealous they are of our relationship."

Do you see how absurdity can loosen things up a bit?

Make Sure You Aren't Being Forced

If the person still feels unsure whether force is being used, there are two great comebacks that I recommend. Watch how Chris followed with both of them.

> Chris: "Do I have to?" Here, the message is: "*Am I being forced?*"

> Pat: "No, you don't have to, but it would sure make my day if you did!"

Chris: "Yeah, but what if I don't do any of that stuff you just said you want?"

Chris is testing to see whether all the force has been retracted. If Pat comes back with anything that sounds like this behavior is expected, or that it is the *right* way to be, or that there will be consequences for noncompliance, Chris will hit the buzzer again.

Remember to ask either or both of these questions when you aren't sure about the speaker's intentions about wanting you to do something: 1) "Do I have to?" and 2) "What if I don't?" Allow your partner to reassure you that he or she is not using force, and that there will be no repercussions for noncompliance.

The Promise of a Powerful Partner

Pat's response at this point in the conversation will reveal the most crucial aspect of *Powerful Partnerships*®. A powerful person doesn't use force to manipulate an outcome and doesn't punish a person for not delivering what was asked for. Instead, a powerful person promises to handle his or her own upset feelings by telling the truth as many times as it takes until the individual feels better. Watch how Pat answers Chris' last question:

Pat: "If you don't do what I ask, the worst thing that will happen is that I'll probably get upset but I'll tell the truth again until I feel better and get over it."

Chris: "Okay."

Remember, force is in the eye of the beholder. It doesn't matter what you meant; what matters is how your message was received. None of this can be faked. You either feel better or you don't. You either feel forced or you don't. You either forgive the person or you don't.

Are We Done Yet?

Sometimes, in such a conversation, we just want it to be over. We might believe we are done because we have already spent a lot of time on the subject. Perhaps, too, we are embarrassed that it has taken so long for us to get over what was bothering us, and we don't want to admit that we are still stuck holding onto a resentment.

Unfortunately, you can't shortcut this process if you don't really feel complete. Complete means that you have nothing left to say, that all of the four channels have been examined and emptied of their contents. There is nothing else that you feel but aren't saying. There is nothing else that was done or said that bothered you. There is nothing else that you want but haven't asked for. And, there is nothing that was done or said that you appreciate but haven't told them. Sometimes, when I would practice this with my wife, the following dialogue would occur:

Lauren: "Are you complete?"

Jim: "Yeah, I'm over it now."

Lauren: "Great. Then come over here and give me a hug."

Jim: "I just don't feel like hugging right now."

Because of my answer, she knew that I wasn't done and I was not being truthful about being complete. The willingness to give the other person a hug became a pretty good test of true forgiveness for us.

CHAPTER **12**

What to Do and What to Say When You Realize You Are Upset

What you will learn from this chapter:

How to recover from a glitch without making things worse

We've discussed how important it is to distinguish between the truth (how you feel about the facts) and everything else that you could speak of e.g., opinions, suspicions, and beliefs, etc. Our experience is not based solely on the facts but, rather our interpretation of the facts—what we make it all mean. For this reason, two people could observe the very same occurrence and yet have wildly different interpretations of that event and thus very different emotional reactions.

Very often, in relationships, one partner assumes that they know their partner's motives and intentions without ever checking to see if their interpretations are accurate. This is how arguments often begin.

Alice: "What is your problem? Obviously you're mad at me. Why don't you just get it off your chest rather than being passive-aggressive with me all afternoon?"

Fred: "I'm sick and tired of your unsolicited analysis, Dr. Freud! Stop telling me what is happening inside my head! Just back off!"

Alice: "You see? You *are* mad at me. I was right!"

Fred: "I wasn't before but now I am."

Alice: "Oh sure."

What is Alice actually seeing? Is she seeing passive-aggressive behavior? Unless she can separate the facts from her interpretation of the facts, the truth will never come out and it will be very hard for their relationship to heal.

I notice and I imagine

Here's a quick method of keeping these two worlds of experience (fact and fantasy) separate so that arguments can be prevented.

As soon as you notice that something is amiss between you and your partner, say this:

I notice ... (facts). *For instance, I notice that we've been together for an hour and you have only said a few words to me and you haven't made eye contact with me either.*

It's very important that after you say, "I notice..." you only mention observable facts that anyone else might have noticed were they standing at your side.

Then, say, ***I imagine... (anything you wish)***. After you say, "I imagine," you are free to assign any meaning you wish to what you just observed. If you are correct, your partner will probably start telling the truth and the two of you will feel closer for it. Even if they don't respond, you'll still feel better than if you had said nothing because you just told your truth.

The best part of this method is that by not acting on the assumption that your interpretations are correct, you give your partner an opportunity to straighten you out if you are mistaken. Listen to how differently the previous conversation might have gone were Alice to employ this technique.

> Alice: "I notice that we've been together for an hour and you have only said a few words to me and you haven't made eye contact with me either. I imagine you are mad at me and are trying to avoid me. I also imagine you are trying to punish me for something."

Fred: "No, it's not that. It's not even about you. There was a big screw up at work and I'm not sure, but I think I might be responsible for it. I can't stop thinking about it. I'm afraid that everybody's going to be blaming me for it when I get back to work on Monday."

Alice: "Oh. I'm sorry that happened to you. Can you tell me what happened?"

Fred: "The server went down and a lot of data was lost. I may have inadvertently programmed it to shut down because I was working on the scheduler at the end of the day. I don't think I programmed it to do that but I might have without realizing it."

Alice: "Is there anything I can do to help?"

Fred: "No. There's nothing anyone can do now. I'll find out on Monday, I guess."

Alice: "Yeah. I wish I could say something to make you feel better but I don't know what to say."

Fred: "It's okay. I'll get through it somehow. I just wish I knew what actually happened."

Alice: "Thanks for telling me. I thought you were upset with me."

Fred: "No. It's not you."

Alice: "Okay."

The other great thing about this technique is that when you say what you imagine, you can make up any interpretation you want. It gives you an opportunity to advance the most charitable interpretation you can think of rather than one that is suspicious and based on fear. For instance, in an e-mail you could write: *I notice that I have left you several messages and have not heard back from you. I imagine you are crazy busy right now. When you come up for air, give me a call and we'll schedule a time to get together.* This interpretation offers the reader the benefit of the doubt instead of a withering criticism of his lack of responsiveness.

A Few Key Words

Some of the hardest elements to repair in a relationship are words or deeds said in anger. Frustrated, angry feelings can give way to hurtful attacks that tear at the fabric of any relationship. These outbursts are hard to take back, hard to forgive, and often harder to forget. With practice, the use of one key word uttered by either you or your mate can trigger a useful series of memorized responses that can quickly diffuse a potentially damaging exchange and avoid a prolonged argument.

Years ago, a famous quarterback for the Baltimore Colts, Johnny Unitas, used a series of memorized plays called the two-minute drill to score a touchdown in the last few minutes of a game. Because the maneuvers were memorized, the players could carry them out quickly without ever having to huddle and the team would get within scoring range in the shortest possible time. The baffled opposition wouldn't know how to react when, in less than two minutes, Unitas could take his team down field and score. It was highly effective.

You can use the upcoming series of words much like the two-minute drill to keep you from sinking into deep conflict. If you have a partner, memorize the plays as outlined below, and either one of you can invoke these drills when you need them.

Overkill

When your partner is repetitive in order to get you to understand something, you might reach a saturation point after which it becomes difficult to hear the same idea repeated *ad nauseam*. When this happens, use the word *overkill*. *Overkill* alone is a simple way of saying, "Okay, you've made your point. I heard what you said. You don't need to repeat it because I already understand your concern."

Upon hearing "overkill," the recipient has a responsibility to stop talking immediately. It's part of the drill.

In the ensuing silence, the silenced person can take stock of what was said and of whether he or she feels understood. If the speaker feels understood, then he or she won't have any trouble letting go of the conversation and stopping the repetition.

After 30 seconds, if the silenced partner still doesn't feel heard, the individual may say, "I know you said 'overkill,' but I still don't feel like you understood what I was trying to convey."

The partner who invoked *overkill* now has an immediate responsibility to repeat what he or she understood the other to say. If that is successful, the silenced party must drop the topic and avoid a long argument.

At times, the silenced partner might say, "You heard most of it but there is one more part that I don't think you got." He or she would then explain the part of the communication that seemed to be misinterpreted.

Then the partner who invoked *overkill* will repeat back that last part to the listener's satisfaction. The topic is then dropped.

In the past, I have found myself repeating something to my wife because I was convinced she wasn't getting my communication. Whenever she put *overkill* into play, I would wait for about 15 seconds before telling her that I still didn't feel understood. To my surprise, she was usually able to convey back to me exactly what my concerns were. Understanding that, I had no need to keep repeating anything; we were able to move on. Before *overkill* entered our game plan I would have bet money that she had missed my point entirely because of how she was responding to me during the conversation. Not so, as it turned out.

You can learn plenty and save yourself some unnecessary conflict through the use of *overkill*.

Meltdown

Use this key word to avoid saying or doing something irresponsible in the face of extreme upset. Say *meltdown* when you are at the end of your rope, or feeling exasperated, overloaded, full of self-loathing, or pent-up rage. Translation: "I'm starting to lose control of myself, and I can't handle any more input (even well-intentioned, loving concern) at the moment."

Rather than breaking down or verbally/physically attacking whoever happens to be nearby, you say *meltdown*. At this point in the drill, the other person knows exactly what to do. He or she will immediately leave you alone and not try to engage you in any way. Often it is best to give the upset person space to calm down by leaving the room or the house. Or the one who is distressed may leave without protest.

The person who invokes the meltdown drill is responsible for letting others know when he or she has regained composure and is back in control. Don't just leave others guessing as to whether or not you recovered from what bothered you. When you are calmer, you can start telling the truth about what you were feeling or wanting, or what upset you beforehand.

By the way, *meltdown* often follows an incident in which *overkill* should have been used but wasn't; instead, the situation got progressively worse until one of the parties just couldn't take it anymore.

Both key words initiate a drill for either party to save time, energy, aggravation, or worse. They serve to keep the situation from going irretrievably off track. They also allow each person to save face rather than to react in ways both might regret later.

Do-Over

Sometimes a conversation can go off track before either party realizes what is happening. Rather than allowing things to get worse, as soon as one person sees that things are disintegrating, he or she can say, "Could we have a 'do-over'?" If the partner agrees, then the conversation is discontinued immediately. Whoever started the conversation starts it again as if the previous unpleasantness never occurred. Sometimes, for dramatic effect, one person will actually leave the room and walk in again signaling a completely fresh start. Rather than hash out what happened previously, they just begin again, this time telling the truth. The context is changed and an impending argument can be avoided. Asking for a do-over is another way of saying, "I don't want us to argue, I want to be on the same team with you." I almost always say, "Yes" when asked if we can have a do-over and so does Lauren. It feels like hearing the kind of preamble that makes me want to give my partner the "green light" to proceed.

CHAPTER **13**

Regenerating and Recreating Love

What you will learn from this chapter:

How to make love stay

Going the Distance

What does it take to have a long-lasting, committed relationship? Many search for the perfect person—someone who matches their interests, values, body type, sense of humor, religious and political beliefs, level of libido, etc. This isn't a bad idea on the surface. Why not start with characteristics that you like and admire? If you aren't attracted now, chances are you won't become more enamored as time goes by. Many wonderful characteristics, however, don't ensure a successful long lasting relationship; they just provide a better start and more fun in the beginning.

Imagine that you and an acquaintance are both planning separate cross-country road trips. You and your friend have a choice of buying two seemingly identical cars with the same engines. The only difference is that one car has a small battery and an alternator while the other has only this incredibly powerful battery to keep the spark plugs firing and the radio playing. This battery is amazing in that it lasts five times longer then a normal one. In fact, the battery supercharges the car. It starts the engine more quickly, handles many accessories simultaneously, and even makes the headlights shine more brightly. Impressed by this new technology, you choose the car with the high-tech battery. After your friend chooses the other car, you both head out across the country, enjoying the ride.

The trip goes smoothly until you cover 1500 miles. At that point, you notice the lights aren't quite as bright as they were when you started out, and the radio isn't as loud. After you get gas, the car hesitates a little when you start it back up. Eventually, your car dies on the highway. Waiting for the tow truck, you feel disillusioned about your new auto with its incredible battery. You are no longer impressed. "Maybe I should have chosen the other car," you say. Your feeling is reinforced when you later learn that your friend made it across the country just fine with a much smaller battery. Oh, that's right—the other model also had an alternator and yours didn't!

Here's the point: If you have an alternator or a generator, you don't need an incredible battery. The beauty of the alternator is that it gives you the ability to recharge the battery as you drive, allowing you to travel hundreds of thousands miles without ever running out of juice. That's why your friend's battery, though small, never ran down after all those miles. It was being recharged along the way.

Sorry for the extended metaphor, but I'd like for you to consider a committed relationship as you would a long road trip, one in which you would strive to feel great all along the journey, not just at the beginning. While it is wonderful to start out feeling abundant love for your incredible partner and being impressed by his or her terrific qualities, what you need long-term is the ability to regenerate the love you originally felt so that you don't run out of "juice" over time.

Through practice, you'll learn to repair problems that arise along the way. In time, you'll be able to transform little "glitches" into wisdom about how to make your journey with your partner the best it can be. Each glitch will give you a clearer understanding of your partner's boundaries, what to avoid and what to encourage to bring out the best in him or her.

Successful relationships don't happen automatically because you picked the right person. The love you feel along the way and at the end is something that is re-created and regenerated many times over the course of the journey. People who are good at regenerating love keep their batteries charged up; they never worry about their relationships winding down or dying at the side of the road.

CHAPTER **14**

Staying Connected

What you will learn from this chapter:

How to avoid kicking over beehives

One of the best things about being able to tell the truth to your partner and to hear the truth from him or her is that you become clear about where all of his or her "buttons" are. You learn that you can touch your partner in places (the buttons) that guarantee an unfavorable reaction. You glean this knowledge from the instances in which you might have violated his or her boundaries in the past.

I once asked a friend why he didn't talk to his long-term employee about some issue he had with her performance. He said, "I can't do it. Whenever I confront her with anything, she gets all red in the face and looks like she is either going to attack me or start crying." His notion of "let's not go there" is all too common in communication after a bad experience. However, in some cases, you can't just avoid a problem that needs to be resolved. Thus, *Powerful Partnerships*® and The Four-Channel Clearing™ come in handy.

Even if you are able to talk through issues using *Powerful Partnerships*®, you still might not want to focus on certain subjects if you don't absolutely have to when they are especially painful for your partner or arouse defensiveness. For instance, continuing to harp on how the annoying habits or values of your in-laws drive you crazy will probably not be productive even if these are your true feelings. Whatever you focus on tends to increase. Thus, the more you focus on problems such as these, many of which you cannot change, the larger they will loom in your consciousness.

A Repeated Glitch

Bill and Debbie, husband and wife, have gotten into strained conversations during his attempts to help her improve her computer skills. Although he is computer savvy and enjoys teaching others how to use a computer, Bill has a way of tutoring his wife that makes her feel stupid or slow. The result is not pleasant for either of them.

Bill has worked to be more sensitive. However, when he bends over backwards to be kind and patient, Debbie tends to feel patronized. Maybe it's a combination of his teaching style and her insecurity regarding her technical skills, but the dynamic doesn't seem to work for them. Rather than hack away at this, Bill has learned to step back.

When she asks him for help, Bill just fixes the problem on her computer. He makes no attempt to teach her anything. In turn, Debbie is appreciative, which makes Bill glad to help. Also, since recognizing that having Bill teach her is an unfavorable option, she has been picking up most of her new skills on her own and from others. If she does ask Bill a basic question, he answers without trying to teach more than she wants to learn. He made this change out of love, and Debbie receives his response that way.

What If You Have to Push a Button?

With *Powerful Partnerships*® you will get through difficult conversations and become more intimate as a result. By becoming more conscious of boundary violations and where the "buttons" exist, out of your love and respect for your partner, you will learn not to push them. But what about the difficult subjects that you can't stop thinking about? It won't help the relationship to just ignore your feelings. How should you tackle such topics to prevent distance and/or unrelated arguments from arising through your silence?

The best way to deal with touchy subjects is to work hard on your preamble. Establish a context in which your partner won't feel attacked, defensive or hurt by what you are about to say. Assure your partner of your sincere real intentions for bringing up the subject. Wait for the green light before proceeding. Also, keep in mind that when your partner urges you to get on with it, you've done an adequate preamble.

CHAPTER **15**

The Courage to Feel

What you will learn from this chapter:

How heroes are sometimes cowards

The Oedipus Myth

The lessons from the Greek play "Oedipus the King" by Sophocles are especially relevant today. Sigmund Freud, the renowned psychiatrist, saw the story as a metaphor for human sexual development (little boys wanting to kill their fathers and marry their mothers), but it is especially pertinent to understanding why we all are driven to resist fate. The story endures because it reveals the human condition in a way that has compelled audiences throughout time. A brief synopsis of the plot explains:

> When Oedipus is born, a grim prophecy placed upon him says he will grow up to kill his father and marry his mother. Upon hearing this, his father, orders a slave to bind

the baby's feet and then leave the infant on a mountain to die. However, the slave pities the baby. He gives him to a shepherd, who, in turn, gives Oedipus to the childless royal family, the King and Queen of Corinth. The King and Queen of Corinth never reveal that Oedipus was adopted.

While attending a party at 18 years of age, Oedipus overhears someone commenting to another, "Oedipus is a bastard," and for days he is rankled. To resolve the question of his parentage, he consults the Oracle at Delphi. The Oracle tells him about the prophecy—that Oedipus will indeed kill his father and marry his mother. Distraught, he runs away from home to prevent the prophecy from happening.

On the road, he gets into an altercation with an arrogant old man in a wagon who insists that Oedipus yield the right of way. Each one refuses to budge until the old man starts poking Oedipus with his cattle prod. In a fit of ancient "road rage," Oedipus kills the old man and his slaves.

Oedipus continues his travels in which he encounters and defeats the Sphinx, a monster that was plaguing Thebes. The city of Thebes then receives Oedipus as a hero and rewards him by making him ruler. Oedipus is further offered the hand of the previous ruler's widow, Jocasta.

The previous ruler (as you have might have guessed) was Oedipus' biological father, Laius, the man he killed on the road. Now, Oedipus is married to Laius' wife, who is, in fact, his biological mother.

The prophecy has indeed come true, despite—or because of—everyone's efforts to prevent it.

The Self-Fulfilling Prophecy

This story is one of the oldest examples of the self-fulfilling prophecy. The prophecy only comes true because we believe it will (or we're afraid it will) and, in our efforts to prevent it, we actually bring it about.

So what does Oedipus have to do with *Powerful Partnerships*®? As is turns out, when we are young, we catch wind of a different sort of two-part prophecy that we, too, try to avoid.

Such prophesies originate from our relationship with our parents. Parents claim to love us, but they are imperfect. Some apply unkind or unfair treatment. Some can be harsh and judgmental. Others are even abusive at times (in our experience, at least). As a result, we might secretly resolve not to act the same toward our children, if we have any.

This brings us to part one of the prophecy: *You will grow up to be just like your imperfect parents and do unto your children the very things that you swore you'd never do!* The prediction seems especially foreboding in light of personality traits and habits that we find distasteful and annoying in our parents.

What's more, as we grow up, we begin to perceive our parents' relationship with each other in a less idealized way than we did as young children. They may or may not be divorced or estranged, but we see their relationship with all its shortcomings, disappointments, and pretenses. We also resolve not to choose a mate like the one our mother or father chose—and not to treat our partner the way our parents treated each other.

Considering how you might view relationships, part two of the prophecy can also be disconcerting: *You will grow up to marry a person who is much like your opposite sex parent. You will also relate to this person just the way your same sex parent did with his or her mate despite your resolutions to the contrary!*

The common reaction is much like that of Oedipus (or Laius for that matter). Railing against the prophecy, you might have vowed that it won't happen to you.

The notion that your fate is to repeat the mistakes you witnessed as a child is repugnant.

So what might you do? You might have resolved to defeat the prophecy by searching for someone who doesn't come close to resembling the negative traits of your father or mother.

If you felt abused, neglected, or abandoned growing up, you might have resolved to parent differently if you have children. If your parents didn't have much or give much, you might have a tendency to be lavish with your offspring. If your mother was driven and aggressive, perhaps you will seek out someone docile and compliant to marry. If your father was unsuccessful financially, you might seek a real go-getter who will provide well for you (or you may personally strive to become what he wasn't). If your parents were materialistic, you might be more attracted to someone who enjoys the simpler things in life.

Sooner or later just what you hoped to avoid will be visited upon you with your mate and your offspring regardless of (and often because of) your efforts to avoid your fate.

I Married Mom

When I met my wife, I was instantly attracted to her. Much of what attracted me were her characteristics that differed from my mother's. For one thing, my mom never had much food in the house when we were growing up. I remember opening the refrigerator and seeing milk, ketchup, a head of lettuce in one bin, and maybe an apple in the other bin, but never anything fun to eat. In my house, if the refrigerator was stocked with good food it was because my parents were having a party that night, and I was told not to touch any of it. Lauren had a refrigerator stocked with great food, and soon after we started going out, she kept it filled with foods that she knew I enjoyed. Looking back, I thought I had defeated the prophecy right there! She was nothing like the mom from whom I wanted to escape.

What's more, my new girlfriend was like my mother in all the best ways. Like my mom, for example, she laughed at my jokes and thought I was handsome. More importantly, she was fun to talk to, responsible, caring, and physically beautiful.

Everything was fine for a while, but as the "honeymoon" wore off, I came to a terrible realization: Lauren not only shared my mom's worst characteristics, but her traits were ten times worse.

What I couldn't stand about my mother was her capacity to be judgmental. Too frequently, it seemed, she had a critical comment regarding people and situations. Consequently, when she turned her focus on me, I prepared myself to be judged. After a while, her positive judgments of me felt just as uncomfortable as her negative assessments.

In marrying Lauren, I thought that I had escaped my terrible fate—living with a critical woman. She seemed so accepting and non judgmental at first. Soon, however, I began to hear Lauren's frequent disapproval, and the notion that I hadn't escaped anything left me feeling stuck and powerless. I went through a painful, depressing period.

Instead of divorcing her or walking around like a victim, I used what I had learned about *Powerful Partnerships*® to express myself fully, even if I sounded ridiculous, petty, unreasonable and demanding. I learned to express my uncomfortable feelings and desires without resorting to force. As a result, they eventually passed, and I began to feel differently about Lauren and my situation.

Even If You Successfully Resist the Self-Fulfilling Prophecy, You Lose

What happens if you purposely choose a partner who is the polar opposite of a parent? If you end up yearning for the characteristics you hoped to escape, don't be surprised.

I once worked with such a couple. Lucy was the product of a domineering, controlling, successful father. She beat the prophecy by marrying Frank, who would never dominate her or anyone else. Though Frank was not controlling, he was a feckless non-achiever who failed to provide for his wife and children. Resisting the prophecy, therefore, left Lucy with financial problems. In fact, without enough money to pay bills, she ended up having to ask her father to help finance their house.

Lucy's father did even better than that. He bought the house outright in his own name, and Lucy and Frank paid him rent from then on. In the end, Daddy maintained control. Why do you think this happened?

Another client of mine, Jeffrey, grew up with a macho, gruff, bullying father. While in our sessions, Jeffrey described humiliating childhood situations in which his father shamed him and lacked sensitivity. Therefore, as an adult, Jeffrey rejected his father's values and became a "new-age sensitive guy." He could express his feelings, give hugs, cry sometimes, and listen attentively. The qualities served him well in a number of areas, especially in his relationships with his wife and children.

At the same time, by rejecting his father outright, Jeffrey rejected many favorable characteristics that he sorely needed as an adult. For instance, his customers and venders repeatedly took advantage of this "nice guy." Overall, people perceived his gentleness as weakness. He was averse to any confrontation for fear of sounding or acting like his dad, but Jeffrey would have benefited from some of the toughness and confidence exhibited by his father. Again, even though Jeffrey seemed to defeat the prophecy, he brought about other types of conflict in his life.

So What Do We Do?

A particular expression conveys good advice: "Turn around and embrace your demons or they will bite you in the ass."

Face your anxiety, your discomfort, and your fears so that they transform into something else rather than chase you through life. Be conscious of your feelings and tell the truth about what bothers you until you get over it. You'll eventually find that whatever bothered you will have little, if any, impact. If you face and feel your feelings, you can change your fate rather than "acting out" the way Oedipus did.

Oedipus Was a Coward and So Were His Parents

Oedipus was hailed as a brave ruler who conquered the Sphinx and tried to save his parents from a terrible fate. You could also say that he was, in fact, a coward. He didn't have the courage to face his fears and experience his revulsion over the prophecy. Instead of expressing his concerns to his parents, he ran away. In effect, he ran away from his feelings (his demons) for fear that they would force him to act out the prophecy. As it turned out, running away empowered the prophecy to come true.

I have often used the myth of Oedipus to help clients recognize similarities in their own lives. The insights reveal one of the hardest factors to confront about being human: Individuals can feel or behave like animals or beasts in some ways.

Even though we live in a civilized society, we have within us the potential for homicidal rage and inappropriate sexual urges. We may fantasize about killing someone or imagine what sex with an inappropriate partner might feel like, but we don't share these thoughts or feelings with others for fear of what they might think of us. It is important to understand that we all have feelings that could hurt or shock others, whether we express them or not. However, by running away from our emotions and thoughts or "acting out," we are as cowardly as Oedipus and his biological parents.

Writing a New Ending to the Oedipus Myth

Imagine, if you will, a different ending to the Oedipus story. This ending requires true courage, but it doesn't produce as interesting an ending to the story.

As in the old, the new version has Oedipus scared and repulsed by the prophecy. However, instead of running away from his fears, he returns to Corinth to speak honestly with his parents, the King and Queen. Still unaware that he is adopted, Oedipus presents the following unlikely monologue (using contemporary language and the *Powerful Partnerships*® process):

> "Mom and Dad, I just found out about the prophecy that says I'm going to kill my father and marry my mother. It scares and sickens me to think that something like that could ever happen. I thought about running away, but I've decided to stay and tell the truth about how I feel. I'm going to express all my feelings, even if what I say sounds inappropriate and childish. Here's the truth for me.
>
> "Dad, for years, you have been going off on long tours of duty to fight in campaigns, and you leave me alone in the house with Mom. In your absence, I become the man of the house. It isn't easy running things while you are gone, but I've gotten used to my responsibilities. I'm

good at my job, and I kind of like it. Mom relies on me, and I feel that I'm useful. The truth is that I've often fantasized about you dying on the battlefield and me becoming the King with Mom as my Queen.

"I especially hate it when you come home after being gone for two years and just brush me aside to take over where you left off. Who do you think has been running this place all that time without your help? Me! I resent you for waltzing back in here and dismissing me without the slightest acknowledgment of what I've done while you were gone. I'm jealous that you get to have Mom to yourself when I've had her undivided attention for all that time. I also don't like how you treat her or how she changes when you come back. She seems all suppressed. Furthermore, I am once again forced to take orders from you as if I'm a little child. Even though this sounds horrible, sometimes, I do wish you were dead!

"And Mom, you are a beautiful woman. I'm eighteen now and I have to admit I have had fantasies of having sex with you and of us living as husband and wife. I find myself wishing that Dad would never come back. I know it sounds weird, but I am physically attracted to

you whether you are my mom or not. I see how gruff and demanding Dad is with you, and I think I would make a better husband and a better romantic partner. I also believe that you secretly love me more than him—at least you act that way when he is gone."

"Despite my feelings, here's a bit of news for those waiting for the prophecy to come true: While I would like it if you were out of the picture, I'm not going to kill you, Dad. And while I am physically attracted to you, Mom, I'm not going to act on that desire. I know the prophecy says that I'm going to perform these deeds, but I don't see any way it could make me do this stuff if I sit here and refuse to do it, do you?"

A different ending, wouldn't you say? Yet, this would represent a true act of courage, the willingness to admit how he feels—even if it is gross, inappropriate, and uncivilized—and then *not act on these feelings.* Having had such a conversation with his parents, Oedipus might have defeated the prophecy and gone on to live his life making choices from a place of clarity and consciousness.

Without this kind of self-expression, Oedipus is unable to face his feelings, and like all of us, is doomed to act out the prophecy.

That Which We Resist

Think about this time-honored expression: "That which we resist, persists."

Did you ever have a blemish on your face and instead of ignoring it, you resisted it by squeezing it, playing with it, touching it, staring at it in the mirror, and obsessing over it? The act of resisting causes the element to remain with us. Where the blemish would have been gone in a few days if ignored, it now becomes the "little friend" that sticks around for much longer because it was resisted.

If you do not resist your feelings—whether anger, shame, joy, excitement, depression, happiness, jealousy, sexual arousal, or whatever—and, instead, express them fully, you will be able to forgive those around you and also forgive yourself.

That which isn't forgiven has to be resisted; thus, those elements will remain with you.

Many years ago, I confessed to a married coworker that I had a serious crush on her. I admitted that I had been fantasizing about us "hooking up," and did not intend to do anything more about it. I felt that I had to say something. On one hand, I was obsessing about her, and it was getting harder and harder to do my work. On the other hand, I had become her confidant and friend. All along, I had been suppressing my true feelings.

After I told her my feelings, she confessed that she felt the same way about me. She, too, had felt things heating up as we spent more time together. I then made it clear that I was not telling her this as a prelude to having an affair.

After we spoke, an amazing thing happened—I got over my crush! As the feelings receded and normalized, I was thrilled that I had never acted on any of them because I no longer felt that way about her. I stopped resisting my feelings so that they could not control my behavior.

This is a good place to review a primary assertion of *Powerful Partnerships*®:

Self-expression changes the way you feel and often releases you from the expectation that things have to be different for you to be happy. It heals all wounds and allows people around you to change naturally.

In the case of having feelings for my coworker, I used self-expression to transform my lustful romantic feelings into something else. After we talked, a real friendship began. I had no secret agenda and nothing to hide. To this day, we're still good friends. I still find her attractive but have no desire to act on that attraction.

The Bottom Line

Using the principles of *Powerful Partnerships*®, you can identify and express your feelings in ways that are safe and transformative. By giving yourself permission to be unreasonable, demanding, selfish, and petty, you will be able to express your feelings and get over them. It is precisely because you are no longer resisting them that they can finally disappear. That's what Oedipus needed to do but was too cowardly to attempt. He needed to be with (not run from) those uncomfortable bodily sensations associated with jealousy, rage, and inappropriate sexual urges so that they would pass and not compel him to act out. Those were his demons. If we can embrace ours and not resist them, we can set ourselves free.

It's Never Too Late

Even if you resisted a prophecy for years and choose now to confront your parents' undesirable traits in you and your partner, it's never too late to feel the feelings, tell the truth about them, and be released from them. You will not only see your partner in a new, more loving light, but your actions will go a long way toward forgiving your parents for how they were. Additionally, you'll forgive yourself for sometimes being just like them.

CHAPTER **16**

Why We Want What We Want

What you will learn from this chapter:

How to understand the basis of your desires

We Are All Unique

Ever wonder why certain things bother some people but not others? Why do people desire the things they do?

You and your partner won't have all of the same sensitivities, nor will you share all of the same wants. More than a matter of taste or gender preferences, your different needs and desires are influenced by your interpretations of childhood experiences.

It's important to note that our wants and preferences are not the result of what happened to us when we were young. Instead, it is what we do with what happened to us that determines our experience as adults. How we interpret our early experiences and, consequently, make decisions from those interpretations influences our longings and choices later on. When you say to your partner, "I want (x)," your wants are not arbitrary. They are usually based on one of two things from your childhood—what you didn't like and what you liked.

Repairing the Hurts from Childhood

If your childhood was unpleasant, you will probably want someone or something to make up for all the wrongs you think you suffered back then. You might want your boss or spouse to be the perfect parent to make up for what you didn't get as a child. You may want the material things you were denied in childhood or the affection and approval that you never received. If a person seemed to have those loving characteristics when you first met, you would naturally find them attractive.

If your family moved every few years, you may want to live in one place for a long time. You may want to own a horse to make up for the pony you were promised and never received. The list is endless. It's based on the belief that if we could finally get what we didn't get years ago, we could be happy and fulfilled. In many cases, these desires are understandable. The contrast from our experience shows us what our preferences are and shapes our future desires.

Recreating the Joys of Childhood

You might also want the good things you used to have as a child restored to you in adult life. If you had loving parents, friends or teachers, you will want your present relationships to give you the love you used to receive when you were little. This, too, is only natural. My parents had a great relationship and I wanted one, too. There can be problems with this type of thinking, however, if force is used.

Women have often been warned not to marry a "Mama's boy" and men have been advised not to marry "Daddy's little princess." Why are we given this advice? It's because a "Mama's boy" grows up with the mistaken belief that he can do no wrong, that people who love him are happy to serve him, forgive him, and indulge him in whatever he wants. "Daddy's little princess" is used to manipulating her father with adorable looks, tears and whimsical desires. She has been taught to believe she need only express a desire and then repeat her mantra, "Daddy pays." The problem with marrying a person who has had such an experience is that they are likely to expect the same treatment from their spouse. When it isn't forthcoming, their reaction won't be pleasant.

Strong Bonds

Another problem with these marriages is that the bonds between the son and his mother or between the daughter and her father are often tighter than the bonds between the child and his or her spouse. This is not generally healthy for a partnership. In the strongest families, the bonds within the generations are stronger than the bonds between the generations. It's not about who loves whom more. It's that in a healthy family, the bond between husband and wife will be stronger than the bond between husband and his mother and vice versa. The best committed relationships are the ones that put their partnership first.

...And You Don't Have To

Remember, it is okay to want the things we want whether we are making up for some previous lack or recreating what was good, but it's not acceptable to force someone to give them to you. No one owes you that. You aren't entitled to a rescue no matter how badly you were abused as a child. However, if you tell the truth enough, you won't feel like a victim, so you will not feel the need for reparation and rescue. Your wants won't feel like needs or forceful demands.

Powerful Partnerships® encourages you to ask for whatever you want from everyone without using force.

Eventually, you will not need to ask for much because you will realize that, as we said in the very beginning, nothing external to you has to change for you to be happy and fulfilled.

CHAPTER **17**

The Limits of *Powerful Partnerships*

What you will learn from this chapter:

**How to recognize addiction
and what to do about it**

After many years of working as a therapist with couples, I recognized a silent killer that existed in certain relationships. In one situation, this deadly element exerted its insidious influence over people in ways that I, as a therapist, didn't pick up on until it was too late.

In my initial screening, Sheila denied that she had any problem with drinking or using drugs. "Does anyone else think you have a problem with drugs or alcohol?" I asked. She told me, *No*, so I dropped the subject. We proceeded to work several sessions on issues that she had at work with certain co-workers and her boss. I thought we were making progress.

One day, however, she missed her appointment and never called or returned to my office. When I called her work number to check on Sheila, I was told that she no longer worked there. I left a message on her home answering machine, but she still did not call me back.

I later met someone who had worked at her place of employment, and without revealing my relationship with the patient, inquired about Sheila. I learned that she had been fired for repeatedly drinking on the job. I was shocked and also felt foolish for not recognizing that her primary problem was alcoholism.

Addiction is a killer. It can take many forms—alcoholism, drug addiction, gambling addiction, sex addiction, addictive shopping, workaholism, pornography, and others. I know of two marriages that broke up because one member was addicted to windsurfing! (Yes, windsurfing!) The effect of an unmanaged addiction on relationships can be devastating. Addiction can overpower or unravel many of the positive effects of *Powerful Partnerships*®. It can also, of course, kill.

How to Tell if a Pattern of Behavior Is an Addiction

Addictions involve attractions and cravings that are not good for you. You might become physically ill in the short-term or develop serious physical consequences (obesity, liver enlargement, headaches) over time. You might also risk undesirable social or legal consequences. However, regardless of the adverse consequences, you still pursue it.

Similarly, you might pursue a good thing until it is no longer good for you. For example, the casual enjoyment of video games with their stimulating spark of competition turns into spending almost every waking hour on these games. In addition to wasting time to the detriment of work and relationships, you would keep playing despite physical ailments like carpal tunnel syndrome in your wrist and sleep deprivation.

Another aspect of addiction is its capacity to have an adverse affect on your relationships with family members, coworkers, and/or friends. It restricts the level of intimacy you can have with others. For example, I've had clients who enjoyed getting high on marihuana. Although they would say they did not have a problem with the drug, closer inspection revealed that they spent most of their waking hours getting high, planning to get high, figuring out ways to score more dope, and arranging to buy and sell it. Additionally, they rarely spent time with anyone who did not smoke marihuana, and they stopped many other social activities, including being present for their families. If an activity did not involve getting high, including something as basic as eating dinner with their families, it became an annoyance, something they had to tolerate until they could smoke again.

An addiction further becomes a situation in which *the behavior has you; you don't have it*. You might seem to control it periodically through willpower, but the reality is that you can't over the long run. Sooner or later, every determined attempt to stop leads back to that behavior. As the saying goes, "Willpower creates *won't* power." When you try to stop, you realize you can't.

One of my clients gave up drinking for the Christian season of Lent to prove that he was not addicted. In fact, he did not have any alcohol for 40 days, but he started again the day after Easter, and his daily alcohol intake was the same as it was before Lent. In many such situations, the level of addiction will increase.

Another sign of addition is that the continued behavior defies logic. The wife of a gambling addict exclaimed in disbelief, "You gambled away our rent money? That was our last $500! How could you do that?" In effect, his behavior wasn't a reasoned response to circumstances; it was addictive.

Finally, a growing addiction starts to replace many of the simple pleasures in life that used to satisfy you. You might socialize less with friends or stop taking walks. You will find little enjoyment in anything except your drug of choice, and your thoughts tend to center around all of the factors associated with your specific addiction.

What to Do If You Think You Might Be Addicted?

The recognition that you are addicted to something is a huge first step toward treatment. Sometimes, the recognition alone is enough to let you put structure in your life to keep it from getting out of hand.

For instance, I realized that even though I loved to fish, my fishing could easily become an addiction. During a period of my life, I fished at every spare moment. I not only stayed out until dark, but I blew off appointments with clients so I could fish. Often missing dinner to fish, I would keep telling myself that this was the last cast until I saw something jump on the other side of the lake and then would stay out a little longer to cast over there. In time, I was repeatedly breaking promises to my wife and to myself. I neglected my kids, my work, and my obligations around the house. Ironically, however, I wasn't enjoying it as much as I had when I fished less often.

When I finally saw that fishing was controlling me, and admitted this to myself and my wife, I set up ways to manage the activity. I structured my time so that I could fish for fun yet not let it take me away from people who were important to me.

Now, every year during the week of Lauren's birthday, we fly to Florida to stay at a lovely hotel near a fishing pier. My wife loves to sleep late and I love to fish early, so I wake up at five in the morning and fish until 10:30. She's happy that I let her sleep and I'm happy to have been fishing without concern that I am neglecting my wife. By managing my time in this way, I make sure that my fishing doesn't interfere with our relationship. Lauren trusts me to keep my word, and I get to indulge my passion without guilt. We are both happy this way. It took quite a bit of effort to work out an elegant plan that met both of our needs. Fortunately, we had *Powerful Partnerships*® to help us express ourselves toward that end.

What If You Can't Handle It Yourself?

You would not be alone if you found that identifying the addiction isn't enough to motivate you to stop indulging in it. Frankly, if it's a true addiction, recognition alone probably won't change your behavior. You and your partner would both need to get professional help, either from a drug counselor or an addiction treatment program. For alcohol or substance abuse problems, treatment centers specialize in helping individuals detoxify. Programs further work to help addicts learn to avoid and manage their addictions. Commonly using Alcoholics Anonymous as their treatment model, specialists view addiction as a disease that can't be cured but can be managed effectively so that recovering addicts lead happy, healthy lives. There are other programs that also claim to be successful in treating addictive behavior.

It is extremely important that partners of addicts learn how to deal with their separate role in the addiction, even if they aren't using drugs, gambling, or drinking, etc. An invaluable resource to many individuals and families is the Al-Anon program, designed to help those who are close to the addict manage their own lives without trying to control the addict's behavior.

It is sometimes helpful to seek professional help for recognizing how the behavior is a problem in your relationship and for guidance in deciding what to do about it. *Powerful Partnerships*® alone, although helpful, will not be strong enough to change most addictive behaviors. Therefore, if any of the information about addiction presented here pertains to you or your partner, take immediate action. Don't let it destroy your life and your relationship.

CHAPTER **18**

Achieving Mastery in Your Relationships Through *Powerful Partnerships*

What you will learn from this chapter:

How you can strengthen and deepen your relationship over time

Briefing and Debriefing

Among the benefits of a committed partnership are The opportunities it presents to practice dealing with difficult situations until you and/or your partner achieve a kind of mastery over them. Every partnership contains easy periods as well as times when feelings of cooperation and love are quickly replaced by hurt, anger, awkwardness, or embarrassment.

By examining and discussing situations in which conflict has occurred in the past, you can often prevent the same negative feelings from occurring the next time a similar scenario presents itself. Additionally, a briefing is useful when you are about to face new situations with no prior history. For example, many couples have no idea what the experience of building a house might be like, but they can express their fantasies and concerns about factors they might encounter to devise ways to handle issues before they manifest.

Briefing

When you know that you are about to encounter a situation that previously felt stressful or has the potential to be stressful, hold an informal briefing with your partner beforehand to discuss the upcoming event. The stressors that you might wish to discuss could include visiting in-laws, reviewing bills or finances, getting cars repaired, moving, hiring contractors, dining out, taking road trips, visiting your child's college for parents weekend, attending sporting events, or an upcoming hospital stay. In the briefing, each of you will say what makes you afraid or gives you concern. The following are examples:

- "I'm afraid that you and your mother are going to get into an argument again."

- "I'm afraid we will end up yelling at each other when we go over the VISA bill."

- "I'm concerned that you'll end up with the guys in the living room and I'll be stuck with your mother in the kitchen all evening."

- "I'm concerned that as soon as we get there you will want to drop everything, immediately, run to the beach and leave the unpacking to me."

Once each of you has expressed your concerns or fears, address them creatively to see if there is some way to handle the situation differently so as to avoid the conflict that might occur.

Briefing Example

Bob and Mary were planning to go to his office party. During their briefing beforehand, Mary said, "When we get to the party, I'm afraid that you will start talking to some couple that I've never met, and you will forget to introduce me. I'll just be standing next to you feeling stupid."

She didn't just make up her fear—it was based on an incident from the past when she felt embarrassed, awkward, and angry at Bob. (It might have happened with a previous partner as well.) The scenario could have easily repeated itself, so they both tried to think of how to prevent that. Bob and Mary eventually came up with a series of hand signals to avoid that scenario.

Mary: "How about this idea? If I notice that you have forgotten to introduce me, I'll put my arm around you and squeeze your hand or elbow, you can use that as a cue to quickly introduce me."

Bob: "Well, that idea is fine if I can remember both of their names, but what if I can't remember their names? How can I introduce you then?"

The two talked further until an idea came to light.

Bob: "If you squeeze my elbow to remind me, and I immediately squeeze yours back, it means, 'Help me out here, honey. I've forgotten their names and can't introduce you.' That's your cue to extend your hand toward them and say, 'Hi, I'm Mary, Bob's wife. I don't think I've met you before.' How does that sound?"

This solution worked well at the party, so they now have a system for avoiding those potentially embarrassing moments.

Debriefing

Debriefing is a way for both parties to look back over what happened during that potentially stressful day or episode, by asking, "How do you think we did?" They can also review any breakdowns "What do you think we could do next time not to have this recur?"

Debriefing is a great way to regroup and get back on the same team while looking for creative solutions to problems. Many couples brief and debrief every few days for a few minutes to make sure they are looking out for what lies ahead, managing their expectations, and staying connected. Debriefings should only occur at a time when you can be reflective; they should not be held in the middle of some other activity or if tensions are high. Couples often debrief on the ride home from an activity or just before they go to bed at night. It doesn't hurt to wait until some time has passed so that you can speak without emotions getting in the way. Each couple and each situation is different. While on vacation, for instance, some couples like to debrief every evening before retiring so that they make the best of each day. The strategy prevents an uncomfortable situation from spoiling the next vacation day.

I once worked with Eric and Christine, a couple who gained a valuable insight over time from a number of debriefing sessions following a recurring event. After several visits to Florida to stay with Eric's parents, Eric and his wife Christine noticed (in their debriefing sessions) that any stay with his parents lasting more than three nights seemed to evolve into some intense confrontation between Eric and his dad. Often times, a lovely trip ended on a sour note because the two men argued about an issue shortly before the visit was over. After the argument, relationships between everyone felt strained so that the entire trip seemed stressful in retrospect.

Eric and Christine weren't sure why this was so, but Eric was loath to work through whatever childhood issues he had with his father. Nonetheless, they agreed to keep the visits to no more than three nights, and the situation improved.

In their debriefing sessions, they noticed feeling disappointed that the visit didn't feel like a vacation. After all, they were in Florida, and the weather was usually wonderful. They concluded that visiting family was neither a vacation nor should it be expected to fill that role. Maybe visiting family was just visiting family and a vacation was something different. By lowering their expectations, the couple found that subsequent trips to Eric's parents were less stressful. They became clear about what a vacation meant for each of them. Christine realized that a vacation meant staying in a hotel room, not in someone's guest bedroom no matter how gracious the person might be. As a result of her desire, they made sure not to stay with friends or relatives on vacations. Instead, they rented a hotel room to themselves with maid service. This made Christine (and ultimately Eric) much happier.

Getting the Drill Down

Briefing and debriefing help you refine the life process. After it becomes natural, you'll approach a kind of elegance in communication as you arrive at workable solutions. With practice, you will both become adept at handling many elements of daily life that you used to find stressful and difficult. You will master a whole range of previously upsetting scenarios. In turn, your partnership will grow stronger as you become more confident of your ability to solve problems collaboratively. The situations that used to arouse stress will feel like easy routines that you have practiced and mastered.

Muscle Memory

When you first learn any new skill, be it riding a bicycle, waterskiing, driving a car, etc., you likely notice an overwhelming number of details to remember. *How can I possibly press the gas pedal, let out the clutch, steer, watch out for oncoming traffic and pedestrians, drive at the right speed, stay in the correct lane, and obey traffic signals all at the same time?*

The good news is that over time, with practice, learned skills become natural to perform without much thinking.

In order to accomplish an activity without giving each separate action a second thought, your body develops what is called, "muscle memory." To drive, you gain a sense of what it feels like to let out the clutch and have it connect with the transmission. Such sensations take the place of extraneous mental work. In time, you can perform the actions involved in driving almost simultaneously while carrying on a conversation with a passenger in your car!

The same is true about The Four-Channel Clearing™. At first it may seem awkward and unnatural to keep figuring out what is true and what is debatable. You may have trouble deciding what you want and then expressing the specifics in ways that seem absurd and non-forceful. You may find it hard to identify the adjectives that accurately describe how you feel. As with anything else, it all gets easier with practice. I can't imagine a day going by when I am not expressing appreciations to my wife. I have become so conscious of how great a person she is and how many thoughtful things she does for me that I often find myself in a state of gratitude when I am around her.

Forgiveness

One surprising effect of practicing The Four-Channel Clearing™ is that you'll gain a definite feeling of having said everything you want to say and finding that you are no longer upset about anything that you resented before. You'll feel restored to a calm place of sanity where you can access the love you have for your partner. It feels warm, secure, and peaceful.

To achieve forgiveness, you'll want to begin with the Preamble FReeWAy until telling the truth becomes second nature. A few years ago, my wife and I noticed that we had reached a point at which we rarely went through The Four-Channel Clearing™. We still have small flare-ups now and then, but have developed the ability to shift automatically into forgiveness with each other. From all that practice in telling the truth, we know exactly what forgiveness feels like (much like a muscle memory) and we can often access it without using the four-channel format.

Not long ago, right in the middle of an argument, I said, "Hey, do you want to just go right to forgiveness starting now?" That time she wholeheartedly agreed, and we were back on the same team. On other occasions, she has said, "I can't. I need to say some more about this before I can let it go." At those times, she was true to herself and said whatever truth she needed to say to forgive me.

CHAPTER **19**

Powerful Partnerships Beyond the Committed Relationship

What you will learn from this chapter:

How to be powerful in all your relationships

Every relationship presents the opportunity for partnership. While it isn't always an equal partnership because of the different roles you might play with others, you may still have the chance to experience the best aspects of partnership, usually found in a committed relationship.

A Shared Commitment to Success

Parents often form partnerships with their children's teachers. Though they occupy different roles, both parent and teacher share mutual concern for the success of the student.

Small partnerships can be formed over the littlest things. For instance, you could feel a sense of partnership with a salesperson going out of his or her way to find what you need to purchase. Because you want to find an item, the salesperson would become your partner in pursuit of that goal. Your words would communicate your wishes without implying that you were owed anything or that the individual *should* be doing this work on your behalf. Clearly, you would present no force. After your transaction, you would state how much you appreciated the person (not the individual's effort) specifically for what he or she did along the way. If you learn the person's name, he or she would likely be your partner again should you ever need help in that store.

Assuming Partnership

The assumptions you have as you enter any relationship will strongly influence whether or not a partnership develops. We often get what we expect! Expect that your interactions will be mutually beneficial, that you will arrive at a win-win solution, and that your relationship will be enhanced by mutual cooperation in whatever you take on. If you do, you will notice that you like the person you are dealing with far more than if you don't hold those presuppositions. Expect each dynamic to go well and anticipate that people will be kind and cooperative. You probably won't be disappointed.

One of the most powerful steps you can take in life is to *assume partnership with everyone.* Let yourself feel what it would be like were that the case.

Appreciate Everyone for Everything

You can make no better use of your time than to express your appreciation to people for the smallest words and gestures they make in your favor. In a short while, gratitude will become your natural attitude toward your partner, your world and your life.

Others who feel your appreciation will want to partner with you before you ask them. Expressing gratitude is the single most powerful action you can take to enhance any relationship. Imagine what appreciation can do to enhance your life.

CHAPTER **20**

Putting It All Together

By now, if you've practiced some of what you've read, you know how to do the following:

- Distinguish observable facts from interpretations, opinions, imaginings, suspicions and beliefs.

- Distinguish what is irrefutably true in your speaking and in that of others.

- Distinguish between the content of your conversation and the context in which the conversation is taking place.

By putting it all together, you can now have a great relationship. Here's how:

1. **Put your relationship first.** Put it before work, before kids, before external family, before friends, before hobbies. Make your relationship the safe platform from which you step out into the world. That means spending time together, doing things together, holding date night or Sunday afternoons or whatever time you choose as *your* time. Make this time sacred; don't let anything get in the way of it. Find little rituals that you can do

as a couple on a regular basis that allow you to spend quality time together.

2. **Promise not to use force in all your relationships.** If someone interacting with you feels force and tells you so, release the person from the force if you can. Figure out what is true for you and say that instead.

3. **Tune in to your feelings.** Notice how you feel when you have different conversations, whether they occur in your thoughts or in your speaking. If a conversation doesn't feel good, find a way to think and speak about the same subject that makes you feel a little better, or change the subject. Allow yourself to feel and express feelings that are childish rather than suppressing them and later acting on them. It's okay to reveal the parts of you that are selfish, petty, unreasonable and demanding as long as you don't force people around you to give in to your childish wishes.

4. **Focus on what you like**. Make it your business to be on the lookout for anything you like, and be grateful for what you notice. This applies to your partner, your surroundings, your friends, your body or anything else you can observe. With your partner, focus only on the aspects of his or her personality or body or mannerisms

that appeal to you; those elements will fill more and more of your consciousness.

5. **Find out what pleases your partner and start doing those things**. Become an expert on what pleases your partner, and when you can, do them to make him or her happy. Do them as often as you can without making it a sacrifice. When your partner does or says something that pleases you, appreciate him or her.

6. **Eliminate sacrifice (and its ensuing double punishments) from all your relationships**. Let love become the only legitimate motivator for doing what you do with each other. Don't agree to things that really aren't okay with you. Instead, tell the person that this would be a sacrifice and see if you can come up with a win-win solution.

7. **Practice successive approximation**. Pick up on any slight movement your partner (or anyone you know) makes in the direction that you like and comment on it by saying, for example, "I appreciate you for emptying the dishwasher," even if the other left the door to the dishwasher open. Eventually, the individual's behavior will be even more to your liking.

8. **Ask for what you want even if it is more than you have a right to expect**. Use absurdity and

humor to get people to see that you know your wants are ridiculous but you still want them.

9. **I notice, I imagine**. When something goes wrong, start by saying what you notice (the facts) followed by what you imagine so that you aren't making incorrect assumptions about what you observed. Try to be as charitable in your imagining as you can.

10. **Learn to forgive via the Four-Channel Clearing^{tm}**. If something happened that still bothers you, wait until you can speak rationally about it. Then carry out the Four-Channel Clearing^{tm} with your partner until you can feel forgiveness for whatever he or she did or said that upset you. Remember never to start talking about what you don't like without first establishing a safe context for the conversation by offering a preamble. Wait for your partner to give you the green light on your preamble before you get into the content of what you didn't like. Tell the truth, the whole truth and nothing but the truth.

11. **If you break your partner's trust, apologize and then work diligently to regain that trust by changing your behavior**. Then speak to the other's concerns whenever a similar occasion arises that might remind him or her of the old

incident. You want your partner to see that you are quite conscious of what you did, of how it made the other feel, and of the way you are using that consciousness to be more communicative and less apt to repeat the offense. Keeping your word and telling the truth restore trust faster than anything.

12. **Express your truth whenever you can**. Let people know how you feel, what you like, what you don't like and what you want. Make sure they know that they don't have to do what you want but that it would please you if they did.

My wish for you is that you practice the principles of *Powerful Partnerships*® in all your relationships. While techniques have been shown throughout this book, it isn't technique that heals a relationship and engenders intimacy. Intimacy is achieved by telling the truth, feeling your feelings, honoring boundaries and taking responsibility for what your words and actions create. I hope you'll take advantage of the coaching available to you through *Powerful Partnerships*® Courses and Teleseminars. If you haven't already done so, you may wish to sign up to receive my blog posts at:

http://drjimgoldstein.com/site/blog/

Feel free to contact me through my web site at any time.

The key to a great relationship is in your hands. I wish you love, passion, forgiveness, peace and great happiness going forward.

Glossary

The following are some important terms as defined by Pow*erful Partnerships*®.

Appreciation – a feeling of gratitude for what someone has said or done or for something that transpired. Appreciations are expressed most effectively in this form: "I appreciate you for... [some fact]."

Content – the particular details of the conversation; who, what, when, where; the nuts and bolts of what you are talking about.

Context – how the relationship or conversation feels; feelings about the conversation or relationship often derived from non-verbal communication e.g., a person's tone of voice, gestures, facial expressions, physical proximity; the setting in which the conversation takes place. Depending on these non-verbal elements, the context can feel loving, safe, hostile, inappropriate, adversarial, collaborative, etc.

Descriptive Reality – anything that we perceive through our five senses; anything we could notice that others would notice as well.

Fact – an objective and verifiable observation; something that a person said or did or something that transpired. Anyone else who witnessed these things would agree that they, indeed, happened.

Feelings – emotions or physical sensations. The most effective way to express feelings is to say, "I feel... [adjective or adjective phrase]." Feelings just are. They don't need to be explained or justified. Therefore, it is unwise to say, "I feel [adjective or adjective phrase] followed by the word *because*. Keep it simple.

Force – feeling coerced, pressured, shamed, or blamed; feeling compelled to behave in a certain way; fearing the consequences of non-compliance; feeling moralistically obligated—that we should do something, we have to, we ought to, we need to, we must; feeling guilty if we don't comply. Force is in the eye of the beholder and has little to do with the intentions of the person using it. The same act or utterance might feel like force to one person and not be perceived that way by another.

Forgiveness – being able to say to a person, "I remember what you did or said that I didn't like but I'm not upset about it anymore. We're back on the same team and I won't need to bring this up again the next time we have a disagreement because I am over it." Forgiveness is often achieved by expressing oneself fully after having one's boundaries violated. It is the ultimate goal of the Four-Channel Clearing™.

Four-Channel Clearing^{tm} – a way to express the truth, the whole truth and nothing but the truth when a person is upset. The speaker tells only the truth of their experience staying within these four channels until they feel better. After the clearing, if done correctly, they will feel more connected to their partner and can forgive him or her.

Glitch – an uncomfortable rift in a relationship, anything in an interaction that makes you step back, troubles you, makes you feel unsure, unsafe, or disconnected; a disagreement that doesn't feel good; an incident leading to a loss of closeness; a misunderstanding that has yet to be resolved; something unforgiven.

Interpretive Reality – our thoughts, beliefs, opinions, suspicions, and imaginings about what we notice with our senses.

Intimacy – a feeling of closeness with another person that develops as a result of knowing and respecting one another's boundaries.

Meltdown – a word that triggers a specific set of agreed upon behaviors designed to avoid intense conflict or violence. If one partner says, "Meltdown," it means, "I'm about to lose control and say or do something we will both regret later." Once the meltdown drill is invoked by a partner, the other person must stop talking and leave the vicinity immediately or allow the other to leave. This gives the upset party time and space to compose him or herself. When the person who invoked the meltdown has calmed down, they agree to return to the scene and let the other(s) know that they are have returned to their normal sensibilities. They then agree to tell the truth of their experience, apologize, if appropriate, and re-establish relationship.

Overkill – a word that triggers a memorized set of behaviors to keep an uncomfortable conversation from escalating into something worse. When one partner is making a point yet keeps repeating themselves and the other partner can't stand hearing it anymore (even if they know their partner is right) the listener says, "Overkill." This invokes the drill that plays out as follows: The speaker has to stop speaking immediately. Often that is enough to calm things down and they can move on. If, after 30 seconds, the speaker does not feel understood, he or she asks the listener to repeat back what they heard. If the listener did understand, the conversation is over. If there is something that the listener didn't fully understand, the speaker will explain it one more time and make sure the listener understood that part of the message as well by getting feedback.

Partnership – acting in one's own enlightened self interest yet keeping an eye on the interests of one's partner; being more committed to creating a win-win solution than in being right or getting one's way; working out a compromise that doesn't require a sacrifice on anyone's part; not doing or saying something that would tear at the fabric of the relationship. In a partnership, when boundaries have been violated, each person works to repair the relationship by telling the truth until forgiveness is achieved.

Power – the ability to achieve your goals without resorting to force. Instead of coercing others or impulsively acting on their feelings, powerful people express feelings, desires, grievances and appreciations truthfully with the aim of restoring and enhancing relationship. This type of self-expression tends to change how they feel and allows people around them to want to do what they want. Powerful people see love, not fear or force as the only legitimate motivator in a relationship.

Preamble – a brief monologue given before the start of the Four-Channel Clearing™ to establish the healing context of the impending conversation. In the preamble, the speaker expresses the desire to get over whatever he or she is upset about so that closeness can be re-established. He or she assures the listener that only the truth will be spoken, no force will be used. Interruptions are welcome if the listener feels force or can disagree with what the speaker says. The preamble continues until the listener gives the speaker the "green light" to proceed.

Preamble FReeWAy[tm] – an acronym for the procedure used in carrying out a Four-Channel Clearing[tm]. The preamble is given first followed by the FReeWAy— Feelings, Resentments, Wants and Appreciations. The preamble can be seen as the entrance ramp that gives you access to the FReeWAy.

Request – asking for something to be given or done. A request requires a response. The listener will either say, *Yes, No* or will offer a *counter proposal*. Actions happen when a request invokes a promise from the other person and a time by when the requested item will be completed or delivered.

Resentment – something that was done or said, something that transpired that another person didn't like and has not yet forgiven. Resentments are best expressed as part of the Four-Channel Clearing[tm]. In that setting, they are most effective when stated as follows: You did or said something (or something happened)... *and I didn't like it*!

Sacrifice – violating one's own integrity; saying Yes to something that you really don't want to do; agreeing to do or say something because you feel you have to, not because you want to. Each sacrifice yields two punishments later—you punish yourself for acting in violation of your own integrity and you end up punishing the person for whom you sacrificed. Sacrifice has less to do with what you do than how you feel about doing it. Just by admitting that something is a sacrifice, the same act might no longer feel like a sacrifice and doing it will yield no punishment. Powerful partners agree not to sacrifice nor will they allow their partner to sacrifice on their behalf if they can avoid it.

Sticking Your Arms out of the Window – Telling the truth but not "nothing but the truth"; throwing opinions, beliefs, imaginings, thoughts or suspicions into a conversation as if these things were true. Sometimes nothing bad happens when you stick your arm out of the window of a moving train-- at other times this behavior can have seriously negative consequences. The same is true about wavering from the truth when either party is upset. It's safer and much more effective to stick to the irrefutable truth of your experience.

Structure – the agreed upon boundaries and limits of a relationship inside of which people interact. The structure defines the ground rules of a relationship. Parents can set a bedtime for their children and the children can adhere to this rule without necessarily feeling force. Spouses can agree to be faithful and not use physical violence with each other. This helps to create the structure of their relationship inside of which they can choose to live powerfully.

The Truth – something you say that can't be debated, disagreed with, rebutted or challenged by anyone, anywhere, ever; the irrefutable truth of your experience; often expressed as *how you feel about the facts*.

Want – part of the truth of your experience. As a powerful person, expressing what you want is healing in and of itself. It doesn't require an answer, a promise or even a response. It is just a way of saying what is true for you. If someone hears what you want and chooses to comply with your wishes without feeling forced, that is wonderful but not necessary for you to be happy and fulfilled.

About The Author

JAMES M. GOLDSTEIN, Ph.D.

Creator of the *Powerful Partnerships*® program, Jim has helped countless couples uncover and reawaken the love they used to feel for each other with his revolutionary seminars. Once the blockages to love are removed, the original feelings of attraction and excitement come back as if they had never left. His program shows you how to transform your relationship without therapy or marriage counseling. A former therapist and now a dynamic speaker, author and coach, he has demonstrated in his own marriage of 28 years how love and passion can grow stronger with the passage of time when you follow the principles outlined in his program.

Where Do We Go From Here?

Get Jim's Free Video Series

"7 Steps to A Better Relationship"

Each of these videos will add to your understanding of how to apply the principles you just read about in *Powerful Partnerships*®. By practicing these tips and strategies you will be more able to connect with your partner, your co-workers and everyone else in your life.

Sign Up Now at:

www.drjimgoldstein.com/site/free-bonus/

(The Videos are FREE)

Book Jim to Speak

Dr. Jim Goldstein's Presentation
Brings *Powerful Partnerships*® to Life

Watching Jim on stage is entertaining, inspiring and transformational. He presents the essence of Powerful Partnerships® in a way that everyone can understand and enjoy. His animated delivery and self-effacing humor show audiences that you don't have to be perfect to have an incredible relationship with the people you care about.

Jim can speak on a wide variety of topics, each having to do with improving and strengthening relationships to increase effectiveness, productivity and joy both at home and at work.

Book Dr. Jim Goldstein to speak for
Keynote Addresses • Conferences • Retreats
Non-Profit Programs • Leadership Training • Special Events
Everything from a 15 Minute Tfalk to a Multi-Day Retreat

Learn more at:
www.drjimgoldstein.com

The *Powerful Partnerships*® 8-Week Teleseminar

With Dr. Jim Goldstein

Without leaving home you can transform your relationship in less than 8 weeks.

IF YOU HAVE A PHONE YOU CAN JOIN THE WEEKLY TELESEMINAR.

The teleseminar includes:
- A free hour of coaching from Jim
- Eight regular telesessions
- Three Q & A sessions
- Weekly tips and strategies to practice
- Free videos by Jim
- Access to a Members Only website
- Weekly downloadable podcasts of the sessions

Register on-line at:
www.thecouplescourse.com

Private Coaching Sessions

With Dr. Jim Goldstein

Jim is a master coach and can get you back on track faster than you can on your own.

Private coaching will jumpstart your ability to master the principles of *Powerful Partnerships*® and create exactly the relationship you want.

For an appointment and fee schedules call:

301 340-6406

Or E-Mail: jim@drjimgoldstein.com

Made in the USA
Middletown, DE
20 September 2022

10861076R00136